Schenck's Official Stage Play Formatting Series:

Vol. 65

Euripides'

CYCLOPS:

Five Versions

Designed and Formatted

By

Walter Joseph Schenck, Jr.

Schenck's Official Stage Play Formatting Series: Vol. 65
Euripides' CYCLOPS: Five Versions
Copyright © 2020
by Walter Joseph Schenck, Jr.

This is a work of fiction. Names, characters, places, and incidents either are the product of the author's imagination or are used fictitiously, and any resemblance to actual persons, living or dead, events, or locales is entirely coincidental.

ISBN: 9798636871460
Imprint: Independently published

Printed in the United States of America
In Courier New, 12 point

Walter Joseph Schenck, Jr.,

Awards and Accolades

FAPA Award-winning author, Gold, 2014 –
Priests & Warriors
Category: Religion

FAPA Award-winning author, Silver, 2015 –
Shiloh, Unveiled
Category: Religion

FAPA Award-winning poet, Bronze, 2016 –
Thee & Me in a Mellow Thine
Category: Poetry

Royal Palm Literary Award, 1st Place, Gold, 2017 –
Catharine's Horses
Category: Biography

RECOMMENDED READ LIST
Kirkus Book Reviews:
First Voices

RECOMMENDED READ LIST
Kirkus Book Reviews:
Uncle Earl's Doggies

RECOMMENDED READ LIST
Kirkus Book Reviews:
Comprehensive Analysis of the Synoptic Gospels

Critical acclaim, Kirkus Book Reviews:
"Brilliantly existential book" –
The Birdcatcher

FEATURE AUTHOR in Publisher's Weekly:
The Birdcatcher

Royal Palm Literary Award, 2018 1st Place
Escape to Canada, Rendered in Poetic Overtures
Category: General Catch-All

Royal Palm Literary Award, 2018 1st Place
Hamlet, Reimagined
Category: Play

2018 Royal Palm Literary GRAND AWARD
The Dahris Clair Memorial Award for Play
Hamlet, Reimagined

Royal Palm Literary Award, 2018 3rd Place
A Glimpse of Peace on the Journey to Armageddon
Category: Novella

Royal Palm Semi-Finalist Award, 2018
Prometheus, Reimagined
Category: Science Fiction

Royal Palm Semi-Finalist Award, 2018
Prometheus, Reimagined
Category: Fantasy

FAPA Silver Award-winner, 2019
How to Correctly Format A Stage Play
Category: Research

Royal Palm Literary Award, 2019 1st Place
Blemished, The Stage Play
Category: Play

Royal Palm Literary Award, 2019 2nd Place
Tribulations of Yonah, The Prophet
Category: Novella

Nominated for 2018 Florida Humanitarian Award –
Literature

Professional membership in PEN American Central

Professional membership in Dramatists Guild

FSCJ Acting and Directing Credentials

Euripides
Euripides, son of Cleito and Mnesarchus, was born in 480 B.C.E. on Salamis Island, Greece and died in 406 B.C.E. in Macedonia.

Theodore Alois Buckley
Rev. Theodore Alois Buckley was a translator of classical plays and literature. He was an opium addict and an alcoholic. He was born in 1825 and died in 1856.

Michael Wodhull
Michael Wodhull was born on August 15, 1740 at Thenford, United Kingdom and died on November 10, 1816 at Thenford, United Kingdom.

Edward Philip Coleridge
Edward P. Coleridge was born in 1863 and died in 1936 at Buckinghamshire, England. His work is public domain following international law of the country of origin, 80 years after death, establishing public access in 2016.

Arthur Sanders Way
Arthur Sanders Way was born on February 13, 1847, in Dorking, United Kingdom and died on March 25, 1930 in Ventnor, United Kingdom. His work is public domain following international law of the country of origin, 80 years after death, establishing public access in 2010.

Percy Bysshe Shelley
Percy Bysshe Shelley was born on August 4, 1792 in Horsham, United Kingdom and died on July 8, 1822 in Lerici, Italy.

Walter Joseph Schenck, Jr.
Walter Schenck was born on May 7, 1950 in Warrensburg, MO, and currently lives in Jacksonville, FL. Walter is a professional member of the Dramatists Guild of America.

Reference Materials

The following public domain reference books are personally owned by Walter Joseph Schenck, Jr.

The Tragedies of Euripides, Literally Translated or Revised with Critical and Explanatory Notes, by Theodore Alois Buckley, of Christ Church. Vol 1-2. Vol. II. New York: Harper & Brothers, Publishers, Franklin Square. 1857.

The Nineteen Tragedies and Fragments of Euripides, Translated by Michael Wodhull, Esq, In Three Vlumes, Vol. 2, Printed by John walker; T. Payne; Vernor, Hood & Sharpe; R. Lea; J. Nunn; Cuthell & Martin; E. Jeffery; Langman, Hurst, Rees, and Orme; Lackington, Allen & Co.,; J. Booker; J. Richardson; Black, Parry, & Kingsbury; J. Faulder; J. Asperne; and J. Harris. 1809

The Plays of Euripides, Translated into English Prose from the Text of Paley, by Edward P. Coleridge, B.A., Vol I-III, Vol. II. London: George Bell & Sons, York Street, Covent Garden. Vol. II, 1891.

Euripides, With an English Translation By Arthur S. Way, M.A. in Four Volumes, Vol II, The Loeb Classical Library, Edited by E. Capps, Ph.D., LL.D, T.E. Page, Litt. D., W.H. D. Rouse, Litt. D., Published in London by William Heinemann, 1924.

The Complete Poetical Works of Percy Bysshe Shelly. The Text Carefully Revised With Notes and a Memoir by William Michael Rossetti, in Three Volumes, Volume III, London: Reeves & Turner, 83 Charing Cross Road. W.C., 1890

CONTENTS

THE CYCLOPS

Translated by

Michael Wodhull

PERSONS OF THE DRAMA

SILENUS

CHORUS OF SATYRS

ULYSSES

POLYPHEME THE CLYCLOPS

SCENE: The mountains of Aetna in
                                Sicily.

SlLENUS

O Bacchus, for thy sake have I endur'd
Unnumber'd toils, both at the present hour,
And when these nerves by vigorous youth were strung:
By Juno first with, wild distraction fir'd,
Thou didst forsake the mountain Nymphs whose care   5
Nurtur'd thy infancy. Next in that war
With the gigantic progeny of Earth,
Station'd beside thee to sustain thy shield,
Piercing the buckler of Enceladus,
I slew him with my lance. Is this a dream?   10
By Jove it is not: for I shew'd his spoils
To Bacchus, and the labours I endure
At present, are so great that they exceed
E'en those. For since 'gainst thee Saturnia rous'd,
To bear thee far away, Etruria's race   15
Of impious pirates, I soon caught th' alarm,
And sail'd in quest of thee with all my children:
Myself the stern ascended, to direct
The rudder, and each Satyr plied an oar
Till ocean's azure surface with white foam   20
Was cover'd; thee, O mighty King, they sought.
Near Malea's harbour as the vessel rode,
An Eastern blast arose, and to this rock
Of Aetna, drove us, where the Sons of Neptune,
The one-ey'd Cyclops, drench'd with human gore,   25
Inhabit desert caves; by one of these
Were we made captives, and beneath his roof
To slavery are reduc'd. Our Master's name
Is Polypheme; instead of Bacchus' orgies
We tend the flocks of an accursed Cyclops.   30
My blooming Sons, on yonder distant cliffs,
Feed the young lambs; while I at home am station'd
The goblet to replenish, and to scrape
The rugged floor; to this unholy lord,
A minister of impious festivals: 35
And now must I perform the task assign'd
Of cleansing with this rake the filthy ground,
So shall the cave be fit for his reception,
When with his flocks my absent Lord returns.
But I already see my Sons approach,   40
Their fleecy charge conducting. Ha, what means
This uproar? would ye now renew the dance

Of the Sicinnides, as when ye form'd
The train of amorous Bacchus, and assembled,
Charm'd by the lute, before Althaea's gate?   45

CHORUS, SILENUS

CHORUS
O D E.
I.

Sprung from an untainted race,
Hardy Father of the fold,
Why, bounding o'er that craggy space,
Roam'st thou desperately bold,
Far from the refreshing gale,   50
The verdant herbage of the mead,
And sloping channel wont to feed
Thy trough with springs that never fail?
Yon caves with bleating lambkins ring,
Come, depasture with the flock;   55
Leave, O leave the dewy rock,
Ere this ponderous stone I fling.
Thee with speeding horns I call
To the Cyclops' lofty stall.

II.

Thou too those swollen udders yield,   60
That thy young ones may be fed,
Who, while thou browsest o'er the field,
Lie neglected in the shed;
Slumbering all the live-long day
At length with clamorous plaints they wake,   65
Thou t' appease them wilt forsake
Aetna's vallies ever gay.
Young Bromius and his jocund rout
Here their orgies ne'er repeat,
No thyrsus waves, no drums they beat;   70
Where the gurgling currents spout,
Here no vineyards yield delight,
Nor sport the Nymphs on Nyssa's height.

III.

Yet here I chant the strains which Bacchus taught,
To that Venus whom I sought   75
When with the Maenades I rang'd
Where, gentle Evan, dost thou tread
Alone, and from thy comrades far estrang'd,
Those auburn ringlets floating from thy head?

Thy votary once, hut now a slave   80
To yonder one-ey'd Cyclops, I abide
        In this detested cave:
    Cover'd with a goat's vile hide,
    Thy Friend, alas, expos'd to scorn
    Wanders helpless and forlorn.   85

                        SILENUS
My sons, be silent: bid your followers drive
Their flocks into the stony cave.

                        CHORUS
                    Proceed.
But wherefore, O my Father, in this haste?

                        SILENUS
    A Grecian vessel, stranded on the coast,
I see, and to this cave the mariners   90
Attend their leader, on their heads they bear
Those empty vessels which express they want
Provisions, with fresh water too their urns
Would they replenish. O unhappy strangers!
Who are they? unappris'd what Lord here rules,   95
Dread Polypheme, they in an evil hour
Are entering this inhospitable threshold,
And rushing headlong e'en into the jaws
Of this fierce Cyclops, gorg'd with human flesh.
But interrupt me not; I will enquire   100
Whence to Sicilian Aetna's mount they came.

                ULYSSES, SILENUS, CHORUS

                        ULYSSES
    Can ye direct me, strangers, where to find
Fresh springs to slake our thirst; or who will sell
Food to the hungry sailor? But what means
That groupe of Satyrs, whom before yon cave   105
I see assembled? we at Bacchus' city
Seem to have landed. Thee, the elder-born,
Thee first I hail.

                        SILENUS
        Hail! foreigner; acquaint us
Both who you are, and from what realm you came.   110

                        ULYSSES
    Ulysses king of Ithaca, and th' isle

Of Cephalenè.

                    SILENUS
     That loquacious man,
The crafty brood of Sisiphus, full well
I know.   115

                    ULYSSES
     Reproach me not, for I am he.

                    SILENUS
     Whence sail'd you to Sicilia?

                    ULYSSES
     From the shores
Of blazing Ilion, from the war of Troy,

                    SILENUS
     What, knew you not the way to your own country?   120

                    ULYSSES
     The tempests violently drove me hither.

                    SILENUS
     By Heaven, your fortunes are the same with mine.

                    ULYSSES
     What, cam'st thou hither too against thy will?

                    SILENUS
     Yes, in pursuit of those accursed pirates
Who seiz'd on Bromius.   125

                    ULYSSES
     But what land is this,
And by what men inhabited?

                    SILENUS
     This mountain,
Call'd Aetna, overlooks Sicilia's plains.

                    ULYSSES
     Where are the fortresses and lofty towers   130
Which guard its peopled cities?

                    SILENUS
     They exist not.

No men, O stranger, on these summits dwell.

ULYSSES

But who possess the land, a savage race
Of beasts?

SILENUS

The Cyclops occupy these caves,
They have no houses.

ULYSSES

Govern'd by what chief?
Is this a mere democracy?

SILENUS

They lead
The life of shepherds, and in no respect
Yield to each other.

ULYSSES

Do they sow the'grain
Of Ceres, or on what do they subsist?

SILENUS

On milk, on cheese, and on their sheep, they feed.

ULYSSES

Affords the vine, nectareous juice, the drink
Bacchus invented?

SILENUS

No such thing: they dwell
In an ungrateful soil.

ULYSSES

But do they practise
The rites of hospitality, and hold
The stranger sacred?

SILENUS

They aver the flesh
Of strangers is a most delicious food.

ULYSSES

What said'st thou, banquet they on human flesh?

                    SILENUS
Here no man lands who is not doom'd to bleed.

                    ULYSSES
Where is this Cyclops, in the cave?

                    SILENUS
                  He went
To Aetna's summit, with his hounds to trace
The savage beasts.   160

                    ULYSSES
            But know'st thou by what means
We from this this region may escape?

                    SILENUS
            I know not.
But, O Ulysses, I'll do every thing
To serve you.   165

                    ULYSSES
      Sell us bread, supply our want.

                    SILENUS
I told you we have nothing here but flesh.

                    ULYSSES
  By this, sharp hunger, which makes all things sweet,
May be assuag'd.

                    SILENUS
            Cheese from the press, and milk   170
Of heifers too.

                    ULYSSES
      Produce them: while the day
Yet lasts, should we conclude our merchandise.

                    SILENUS
With how much gold will you repay me? speak.

                    ULYSSES
No gold I bring, but Bacchus' cheering juice.   175

                    SILENUS
  My dearest friend, you mention what we long
Have stood in need of.

ULYSSES
　　This enchanting liquor
Did Moron, offspring of the courteous God,
On us bestow.

SILENUS
　　Whom erst, while yet:a boy
I in these arms sustain'd.

ULYSSES
　　The son of Bacchus,
T' inform thee more minutely who he is.

SILENUS
Aboard the ship, or have you hither brought it?

ULYSSES
Here is the cask, old man, which thou perceiv'st
Contains the wine.

SILENUS
　　It hardly is a sup.

ULYSSES
But we have twice as much as this will yield.

SILENUS
A most delicious spring is that you nam'd.

ULYSSES
Shall I first treat thee with some wine unmix'd,
That thou may'st taste?

SILENUS
　　Well-judg'd: this specimen
Soon will induce me to conclude the purchase.

ULYSSES
A cup too I have brought as well as cask.

SILENUS
Pour forth, that I may drink, and recollect
The grateful taste of wine.

ULYSSES
　　Look there.

SILENUS

       Ye Gods!
How beauteous is its odour!

ULYSSES

Hast thou seen it?

SILENUS

  By Jove I have not, but I smell its charms.

ULYSSES

Taste, nor to words alone confine thy praise.

SILENUS

  Ha! ha! now Bacchus to the choral dance
Invites me.

ULYSSES

   Hath it moisten'd well thy palate?

SILENUS

  So well as e'en to reach my fingers' ends.

ULYSSES

Beside all this, shall money too be thine.

SILENUS

Empty the vessel, and reserve your gold.

ULYSSES

Bring forth the cheese and lambs.

SILENUS

    That will I do,
Regardless of my Lord, because I wish
To drain one goblet of this wine, and give
The flocks of all the Cyclops in its stead.
I'd from Leucadè, when completely drunk,
Into the ocean take a lover's leap,
Shutting my eyes. For he who, when he quaffs
The mantling bowl, exults not, is a madman.
Thro' wine new joys our wanton bosoms fire,
With eager arms we clasp the yielding fair,
And in the giddy dance forget each ill
That heretofore assail'd us. So I kiss
The rich potation; let the stupid Cyclops
Weep with that central eye which in his front

Glares horribly.   225

                              (Exit SILENUS.)

                          CHORUS
          Attend: for we must hold
A long confabulation, O Ulysses.

                          ULYSSES
  We meet each other like old friends.

                          CHORUS
             Was Troy
By you subdued? was Helen taken captive?   230

                          ULYSSES
  And the whole house of Priam we laid waste.

                          CHORUS
    When ye had seiz'd on that transcendent fair,
Did ye then all enjoy her in your turn,
Because she loves variety of Husbands?
False to her vows, when she the painted greaves   235
Around the legs of Paris, on his neck
The golden chain, beheld, with love deep smitten
From Menelaus, best of men, she fled.
Alt would to Heaven no women had been born
But such as were reserv'd for my embraces.   240

             SILENUS Returning, ULYSSES, CHORUS

                          SILENUS
    Here, King Ulysses, is the shepherd's food:
Banquet on bleating lambs, and bear away
As many curdled cheeses as you can;
But from these caverns with your utmost speed
Depart, when ye have given me in return   245
The clustering vine's rich juice which Bacchus loves.

                          ULYSSES
    The Cyclops comes. What shall we do? Old man,
We are undone, Ah, whither can we fly?

                          SILENUS
  Ye may conceal yourselves beneath that rock.

                         ULYSSES
    Most dangerous is the scheme thou bast propos'd,   250
To rush into the toils.

                         SILENUS
         No danger truly;
For in this rock is many a hiding place.

                         ULYSSES
    Not thus: indignant Troy might groan indeed
If from a single arm we basely fled.   255
Oft with my shield against a countless band
Of Phrygians have I fought. If we must die,
Let us die nobly? or with life maintain
The fame we erst in dubious fields acquir'd.

        POLYPHEME, SILENUS, CHORUS, ULYSSES

                        POLYPHEME
    What mean these transports, this insensate uproar,   260
These Bacchanalian orgies? Nyssa's God,
The brazen timbre, and the rattling drum,
Are distant from these regions. In the cave
How fare the new-yean'd lambkins? do they suck,
Or follow they the ewes? have ye prepar'd   265
In wicker vats the cheeses? No reply?
This club shall make ye weep forthwith. Look up,
Not on the ground.

                         CHORUS
            We lift our dazzled eyes
To Jove himself; I view the twinkling stars   270
And bright Orion.

                        POLYPHEME
         Is my dinner ready?

                         CHORUS
    It is. Prepare your jaws for mastication.

                        POLYPHEME
    Are the bowls fill'd with milk?

                         CHORUS
            They overflow,   275
And you may drink whole hogsheads if you will.

POLYPHEME
Of sheep, or cows, or mixt?

CHORUS
Whate'er you please;
But swallow not me too.

POLYPHEME
No certainly;
For ye would foot it in my tortur'd paunch,
And kill me with those antics. But what crowd
Behold I in the stalls? Some thieves or pirates
Are landed: at the mouth of yonder cave
The lambs are bound with osiers, on the floor
The cheese-press scatter'd lies, and the bald head
Of this old man is swoll'n with many bruises.

SILENUS
An me into a fever I am beaten.

POLYPHEME
By whom, old man, who smote thy hoary head?

SILENUS
O Cyclops, by these ruffians whom I hinder'd
From carrying off their plunder.

POLYPHEME
Know they not
I am a God sprung from the blest immortals?

SILENUS
All this I told them, yet they seiz'd your goods,
Eat up your cheese without my leave, dragg'd forth
The lambs, declar'd they would exhibit you
In a huge collar of three cubits long,
Closely imprison'd, and before that eye,
Which in the centre of your forehead glares,
Bore out your entrails, soundly scourge your hide,
Then throw you into their swift vessel's hold
Tied hand and foot, and sell you, with a lever
To heave up ponderous stones, or to the ground
Level some door.

POLYPHEME
Indeed! go whet the knives
Without delay, collect a mighty pile

Of wood, and light it up with flaming brands,
They shall be slain immediately, and broil'd
To satisfy my appetite with viands
Hot from the coals. The rest shall be well sodden;
For I am sated with unsavoury beasts,
Enough on lions have I banqueted
And stags that haunt this mountain: but 'tis long
Since human flesh I tasted.

SILENUS

My dread lord,
Variety is sweet: no other strangers
Have reach'd of late these solitary caves.

ULYSSES

O Cyclops, hear the strangers also speak,
In their defence. We, wanting to buy food,
Came to your caverns from our anchor'd bark.
These lambs to us he barter'd for our wine,
And of his own accord, when he had drank,
Yielded them up; no violence was us'd:
But the account he gives is utter falshood,
Since he was caught without your privity
Vending your goods.

SILENUS

I? curses on your head!

ULYSSES

If I have utter'd an untruth.

SILENUS

By Neptune
Your Sire, O Cyclops, by great Triton, Nereus,
Calypso, Nereus' Daughters, by the waves,
And all the race of fishes, I protest,
Most beauteous Cyclops, my dear little lord,
I sold not to the foreigners your goods;
May swift perdition, if I did, o'ertake
These sinners here, my children, whom I love
Beyond expression.

CHORUS

Curb. thy tongue: I saw thee
Vending thy lord's possessions to the strangers;
If I speak falshood, may our Father perish!
But injure not these foreigners.

POLYPHEME
                  Ye lie;
For I in him much rather would confide
Than Rhadamanthus, and pronounce that he
Is a more upright judge. But Ito them
Some questions would propose. Whence sail'd strangers?
Where is your country and your native town?

ULYSSES
     We in the realms of Ithaca were born;
But after we had laid Troy's bulwarks waste,
O Cyclops, by those howling winds which raise
The ocean's boisterous surges, to your coast
Our vessel was impell'd.

POLYTHEME
               Are ye the men
Who worthless Helen's ravisher pursued
To Ilion's turrets on Seamander's bank?

ULYSSES
   The same: most dreadful toils have we endued.

POLYPHEME
   Dishonourable warfare; in the cause
Of one vile woman, ye to Phrygia sail'd.

ULYSSES
     Such was the will of Jove; on no man charge
The fault. But we to you, O generous Son
Of Ocean's God, our earnest prayers address,
Nor fear with honest freedom to remonstrate
That we your hapless friends, who to these caves
For refuge fly, deserve not to be slain
To satiate with accursed human food
Your appetite: for to your Sire, great King,
Full many a temple on the shores of Greece
Have we erected; Taenarus' sacred haven
To him remains inviolate, the cliff
Of Malea, Sunium for its silver mines
Renown'd, on whose steep promontory stands
Minerva's time, and the Gerastian bay.
But those intolerable wrongs which Greece
From Troy had suffer'd, could we not forgive.
Our triumph interests you, who in a land
With Greece connected, dwell, beneath the rock
Of flaming Aetna. Let those public laws

Which all mankind obey, on you prevail
To change your ruthless purpose, and admit
Your suppliants to a conference, who have long,
Endur'd the perils of the billowy deep;
With hospitable gifts, and change of raiment
Assist us, nor affix our quivering limbs
On spits, to sate your gluttony. Enough
Hath Priam's land depopulated Greece,
Whole myriads have in fighting fields been slain;
The widow'd bride, the aged. childless matron,
And hoary sire, bath Troy made ever wretched.
But if you burn, and at your hateful feasts
Devour the scatter'd relics of our host,
Whither shall any Grecian torn? but listen
To my persuasion, Cyclops, and control
Your gluttony. What piety enjoins,
Prefer to this defiance of the Gods:
For ruin oft attends unrighteous gain.

SILENUS
    Leave not the smallest morsel of his flesh;
Take my advice, and if you eat his tongue,
You certainly, O Cyclops, will become
A most accomplish'd orator.

POLYPHEME
                Vile caitiff,
Wealth is the deity the wise adore,
But all things else are unsubstantial boasts,
And specious words alone. I nought regard,
Those promontories sacred to my Sire.
Why dost thou talk of them? I tremble not,
O stranger, at the thunderbolts of Jove,
Him I account not a more powerful God
Than I am, nor henceforth will heed him: hear
My reasons; when he from the skies sends down
The rain, secure from its inclemency
Beneath this rock I dwell, and make a feast
On roasted calves, or on the savage prey,
Stretcht at my length supine, then drain a pitcher
Of milk, and emulate the thunder's sound.
When Thracian Boreas pours his flaky showers,
In hides of beasts my body I enwrap,
Approach the fire, nor heed the pelting snows.
Compell'd by strong necessity, the ground
Produces grass, and nourishes my herds,
Whom, to no other God except myself,

And to this belly, greatest of the Gods,
I sacrifice. Because each day to eat,
To drink, and feel no grief, is bliss supreme,
The Heaven, the object of the wise man's worship.
1 leave those gloomy law-givers to weep,   425
Who by their harsh impertinent restrictions
Have checker'd human life; but will indulge
My genius, and devour thee. That my conduct
May be exempt from blame, thou shalt receive
As pledges of our hospitality   430
The fire, and that hereditary cauldron
Well heated, which shall boil thy flesh: walk in,
Ye shall adorn my table, and produce
Delicious meals to cheer my gloomy cave,
Such as a God can relish,   435

ULYSSES

I have 'scap'd,
Alas, each danger at the siege of Troy,
'Scap'd the tempestuous ocean; but in vain
Attempt to soften the unpitying heart
Of him who spurns all laws. Now, sacred Queen,   440
Daughter of Jove, now aid me, O Minerva.
For I such perils as far, far exceed
My Phrygian toils, encounter: and, O Jove
Dread guardian of each hospitable rite,
Who sitt'st enthron'd above the radiant stars,   445
Look down: for if thou view not this, tho' deem'd
Omnipotent, thou art a thing of nought.

(Exeunt POLYPHEME,
ULYSSES, and
SILENUS.)

SEMICHORUS I.

That insatiate throat expand,
Boil'd and roast are now at hand
For thee, O Cyclops, to devour: 450
From the coals in evil hour.
Yet reeking, shall thy teeth divide
The limbs of each unhappy guest,
To thy table serv'd when drest
In dishes form'd of shaggy hide.   455
O betray me not, my friend,
For I on you alone depend:
Now approach the shades of night,
Launch the bark, and aid our flight.

SEMICHORUS II.

Thou cave, and ye unholy rites,
Adieu, the Cyclops' curst delights,
Who on his prisoners wont to feed,
Hath banish'd pity from his breast.
Inhuman execrable deed!
On his own hearth, the suppliant guest,
Regardless of the Lares' guardian powers,
Now he slays, and now devours:
Hot from the coals, with odious jaws,
Human flesh the miscreant gnaws.

ULYSSES, CHORUS

ULYSSES

How, mighty Jove! shall I express myself?
The dreadful scenes I in the cave have view'd
Are so astonishing, they more resemble
Some fable than the actions of a man.

CHORUS

What now, Ulysses, on your lov'd companions.
Feasts this most impious Cyclops?

ULYSSES

Two, the fattest,
Having well view'd, and pois'd them in his hands—

CHORUS

How did you .bear, O miserable man,
These cruel outrages?

ULYSSES

Soon as we entered
The rocky cave, he lighted first the fire,
On the wide blaze heap'd trunks of lofty oaks,
A load sufficient for three wains to bear;
Then near the flaming hearth, upon the ground,
Arrang'd his couch of pine leaves, fill'd a bowl,
Holding about ten firkins, with the milk
Of heifers, and beside it plac'd a jug
Adorn'd with ivy, the circumference seem'd
Three spacious ells, the depth no less than four
Then made his cauldron bubble, and reach'd down
Spits burnt at the extremities, and polish'd
Not with a knife, but hatchets; Aetna furnish'd
Such instruments for sacrifice, the stems

Of thorn. No sooner had the hellish cook
Finish'd his preparations, than he seiz'd   495
Two of my valiant comrades, whom he slew
With calm deliberation; one he cast
Into the hollow cauldron; from the ground
Then lifting up his fellow by the foot
Dash'd out his brains against the pointed rock;   500
Severing his, mesh with an enormous knife,
Part at the fire he roasted, and to boil,
His other joints into the cauldron threw.
But I, tho' from these eyes full many a tear
Burst forth, approach'd the Cyclops, and on him   505
Attended, while my friends, like timorous birds
1 urk'd in the distant crannies of the rock,
And all the blood forsook their pallid frame.
When sated with his feast the monster lay
Supine, and snor'd, a thought by Heaven inspir'd   510
Enter'd this bosom; having fill'd a cup
With Martin's juice unmingled, I to him
Bore it, that he might drink; and cried, "Behold
"O Cyclops, Son of Neptune, how divine
"The beverage which our Grecian vineyards yield,   515
"The stream of Bacchus." But already glutted
With his abominable food, he seiz'd
And emptied the whole bumper at one draught,
Then lifting up, in token of applause,
His hand; "O dearest stranger," he exclaim'd,   520
"To a delicious banquet thou hast added
"Delicious wine." Perceiving he grew merry
I plied him with a second cup, well knowing
That wine will stagger him: he soon shall feel
Such punishment as he deserves. He sung;   525
I pour'd forth more and more, to warm his bowels
With strong potations: 'midst my weeping crew
He makes the cave with unharmonious strains
Re-echo. But I silently came forth,
And, if ye give consent, design to save   530
You, and myself. Say therefore, will ye fly
From this unsocial monster, and reside
With Grecian maids beneath the roofs of Bacchus.
Your Sire within approves of these proposals:
But now grown feeble and o'ercharg'd with wine,   535
Attracted by the- goblet, as if bird-lime
Had smear'd his wings, he wavers. But with me,
Do thou, preserve thyself; for thou art young:
And I to Bacchus, to thy antient friend
Far different from this Cyclops, will restore thee.   540

CHORUS
  My dearest friend, O could we see that day,
And 'scape yon impious monster! for we long
Have been depriv'd of the enlivening bowl,
Nor entertain a single hope of freedom.

ULYSSES
  Now hear the means by which I can requite
This odious savage, and thou too may'st 'scape
From servitude.

CHORUS
       Speak, for we should not hear
The sound of Asia's harp with more delight,
Than the glad tidings of the Cyclops' death.

ULYSSES
  By wine enliven'd, he resolves to go
And revel with his brethren,

CHORUS
     I perceive
You mean to seize and kill him when alone,
By some enchantment, or to dash him headlong
From the steep rock.

ULYSSES
    I have no such design
As these: on craft alone my plan depends.

CHORUS
  How then will you proceed: For we long since
Have heard that you for wisdom are renown'd.

ULYSSES
  I will deter him from the feast; and say
He must not portion out among the Cyclops
This liquor, but reserve it for himself
And lead a joyous life: when overcome
By Bacchus' gifts he sleeps, this sword shall point
An olive pole, which to my purpose suited
Lies in the cave: I in the fire will heat,
And, when it flames, direct the hissing brand
Full on the Cyclops' forehead, to extinguish
The orb of sight. As when some artist frames
A nautic structure, he by thongs directs
The pondrons augre; thus will I whirl round

Within the Cyclops' eye the kindled staff,
And scorch his visual nerve.

                    CHORUS
              Ho! I rejoice;   575
This blest invention almost makes me frantic.

                    ULYSSES
     Thee, and thy friends, and thy decrepid Sire,
This done, aboard my vessel will I place,
And from this region with a double tier
Of oars convey.   580

                    CHORUS
              But is it possible
That I, as if dread Jove were my confederate,
Shall guide the well-pois'd brand, and of his eye-sight
Deprive the monster? For I wish to share
In such assassination.   585

                    ULYSSES
              I expect
Your aid: the brand is weighty, and requires
Our social efforts.

                    CHORUS
              I'd sustain a load
Equal to what an hundred teams convey,   590
Could I dash out the cursed Cyclops' eye
E'en as a swarm of wasps.

                    ULYSSES
              Be silent now;
(Ye know my stratagem) and at my bidding
To those who o'er th' adventurous scheme preside   595
Yield prompt obedience: for I scorn to leave
My friends within, and save this single life.
True, 'scape I might, already having pass'd
The cavern's deep recess: but it were mean
If I should extricate myself alone,   600
False to the faithful partners of my voyage.

                              (Exit ULYSSES.)

CHORUS

Who first, who next, with steadfast hand
Ordain'd to guide the flaming brand,
The Cyclops' radiant eye shall pierce?

SEMICHORUS I.

Silence! for from within a song   605
Bursts on my ear, in tuneless verse,
Insensate minstrel, doom'd ere long
This luxurious meal to rue,
He staggers from yon rocky cave.
Him let us teach who never knew   610
How at the banquet to behave,
Outrageous and unmanner'd hind,
Soon shall he totally be blind.

SEMICHORUS II.

Thrice blest is he, in careless play
'Midst Bacchuss' orgies ever gay,   615
Stretcht near the social board whence glides
The vine's rich juice in purple tides,
Who fondly clasps with eager arms
The consenting virgin's charms;
Rich perfumes conspire to shed   620
Sweetest odours on his head,
While enamour'd of the fair
He wantons with her auburn hair.
But hark! for surely 'tis our mate
Exclaiming, "Who will ope the gate?"   625

POLYPHEME, ULYSSES, SILENUS, CHORUS

POLYPHEME

Ha! ha! I am replete with wine, the banquet
Hath cheer'd my soul: like a well-freighted ship
My stomach's with abundant viands stow'd
Up to my very chin. This smiling turf
Invites me to partake a vernal feast   630
With my Cyclopean brothers. Stranger, bring
That vessel from the cave.

(Exit ULYSSES.)

CHORUS

                With bright-ey'd grace
Our master issues from his spacious hall;
(Some God approves—the kindled torch—) that form   635

Equals the lustre of a blooming nymph
Fresh from the dripping caverns of the main.
Soon shall the variegated wreath adorn
Your temples.

(ULYSSES
returning.)

ULYSSES
            Hear me, Cyclops; well I know   640
Th' effect of this potation, Bacchus' gift,
Which I to you dispens'd.

POLYPHEME
            Yet say what sort
Of God is Bacchus by his votaries deem'd?

ULYSSES
    The greatest source of pleasure to mankind.   645

POLYPHEME
    I therefore to my palate find it sweet.

ULYSSES
    A God like this to no man will do wrong.

POLYPHEME
    But in a bottle how can any God
Delight to dwell?

ULYSSES
            In whatsoever place   650
We lodge him, the benignant Power resides.

POLYPHEME
    The skins of goats are an unseemly lodging
For Deities.

ULYSSES
            If you admire the wine,
Why quarrel with its case?   655

POLYPHEME
        Those filthy hides
I utterly detest, but love the liquor.

ULYSSES
Stay here; drink, drink, O Cyclops, and be gay,

POLYPHEME
This luscious beverage, must I not impart
To cheer my brothers?   660

ULYSSES
Keep it to yourself
And you shall seem more honourable.

POLYPHEME
More useful,
If I distribute largely to my friends.

ULYSSES
Broils, taunts, and discord from the banquet rise.   665

POLYPHEME
Tho' I am fuddled, no man dares to touch me.

ULYSSES
He who bath drunk too freely, O my friend,
Ought to remain at home.

POLYPHEME
Devoid of reason
Is he who when be drinks pays no regard   670
To mirth and to good fellowship.

ULYSSES
More wise,
O'ercharg'd with wine, who ventures not abroad.

POLYPHEME
Shall we stay here? That think'st thou, O Silenus?

SILENUS
With all my heart. What need, for our carousals,   675
Of a more numerous company?

POLYPHEME
The ground
Beneath our feet, a flowery turf adorns.

SILENUS
O how delightful 'tis to drink, and bask

Here in the sun-shine: on this grassy couch   680
Beside me take your seat.

                    POLYPHEME
          Why dust thou place
The cup behind my elbow?

                    SILENUS
          Lest sonic stranger
Should come and snatch the precious boon away.   685

                    POLYPHEME
    Thou mean'st to tope clandestinely: between us
Here let it stand.—O stranger, by what name
Say shall I call thee?

                    ULYSSES
Noman is my name.
But for what favour shall I praise your kindness.   690

                    POLYPHEME
    Thee last of all the crew will I devour.

                    ULYSSES
    A wondrous privilege is this, O Cyclops,
Which on the stranger, you bestow.

                    POLYPHEME
          What mean'st thou?
Ha! art thou drinking up the wine by stealth?   695

                    SILENUS
    Only the gentle Bacchus gave that kiss,
Because I look so blooming.

                    POLYPHEME
          Thou shalt weep,
Because thy lips were to the wine applied,
Nor did it seek thy mouth.   700

                    SILENUS
          Not thus, by Jove;
I drank because the generous God of wine
Declar'd that he admir'd me for my beauty.

                    POLYPHEME
    Pour forth; give me a bumper.

                    SILENUS
              I must taste   705
To see what mixture it requires.

                    POLYPHEME
              Damnation!
Give it me pure.

                    SILENUS
              Not so, the Heavens forbid!
Till you the wreath bind on your ample front,   710
And I again have tasted.

                    POLYPHEME
              What a knave
Is this my cup-bearer!

                    SILENUS
              Accuse me not;
The wine is sweet: you ought to wipe your mouth   715
Before you drink.

                    POLYPHEME
              My lips and beard are clean.

                    SILENUS
   Loll thus upon your elbow with a grace,
Drink as you see me drink, and imitate
My every gesture.   720

                    POLYPHEME
              What art thou about?

                    SILENUS
   I swallow'd then a most delicious bumper.

                    POLYPHEME
   Take thou the cask, O, stranger, and perform
The office of my cup-bearer.

                    ULYSSES
              These-hands   725
Have been accustom'd to the pleasing office.

                    POLYPHEME
   Now pour it forth.

ULYSSES
Be silent: I obey.

POLYPHEME
Thou hast propos'd a difficult restraint
To him who largely drinks.

ULYSSES
Now drain the bowl;
Leave nought begind: the toper must not prate
Before his liquor's ended.

POLYPHEME
In the vine
There's wisdom.

ULYSSES
When to plenteous food you add
An equal share of liquor, and well drench
The throat beyond what thirst demands, you sick
Into sweet sleep: but if you leave behind
Aught of th' unfinish'd beverage in your cup,
Bacchus will scorch your entrails.

POLYPHEME
'Tis a mercy
How I swam out; the very Heavens whirl round
Mingled with earth. I view Jove's throne sublime,
And the whole synod of encircling Gods.
Were all the Graces to solicit me,
I would not kiss them: Ganymede himself
Appears in matchless beauty.

SILENUS
I, O Cyclops,
Am Jove's own Ganymede.

POLYPHEME
By Heaven thou art!
Whom from the realms of Dardanus I bore.

(Exit POLYPHEME.)

SILENUS
Ruin awaits me.

CHORUS
Dost thou loath him now?

SILENUS
Ah me! I from this sleep shall soon behold   755
The most accurs'd effects.

(Exit SILENUS.)

ULYSSES
Come on, ye Sons
Of Bacchus, generous youths; for soon dissolv'd
In slumber shall the monster from those jaws
Vomit forth flesh, within the hall now smokes   760
The brand, and nought remains but to burn out
The Cyclops' eye: act only like a man.

CHORUS
The firmness of my soul shall equal rocks
And adamant. But go into the cave
With speed, before tumultuous sounds assail   765
Our aged Father's ears; for, to effect
Your purpose, all is ready.

ULYSSES
Vulcan, King
Of Aetna, from this impious pest, who haunts
Thy sacred mountain, free thyself at once,   770
By burning out his glaring eye; and thou
Nurtur'd by sable Night, O Sleep, invade
With thy resistless force this beast abhorr'd
By Heaven; nor after all the glorious deeds
Atchiev'd at Ilion, with his faithful sailors,   775
Destroy Ulysses' self, by him who heeds
Nor God nor mortal. Else must we hold Fortune
A Goddess, and all other Deities
Inferior to resistless Fortune's power.

(Exit ULYSSES.)

CHORUS
The neck of him who slays his guest,   780
With burning pincers shall be prest,
And fire bereaving him of sight
Soon shall destroy that orb of light.
Within the embers near at hand
Lies conceal'd a smoking brand,   785

Torn from its parental tree.
Maron, we depend on thee;
May th' exasperated foe
With success direct the blow!
May the Cyclops lose his eye,
And curse his ill-tim'd jolity!
Thee, Bromius, how I long to meet
Thy front adorn'd with ivy twine;
Leaving this abhorr'd retreat.
,A1ll, when shall such delight be mine?

ULYSSES, CHORUS

ULYSSES

Be silent, O ye savages, restrain
Those clamorous tongues: by Heaven ye shall not breathe,
Nor wink your eyes, nor cough, lest ye awaken
This pest, the Cyclops, ere he of his eye-sight
Is by the fire bereft.

CHORUS

We will be silent,
And in our jaws confine the very air.

ULYSSES

The pond'rous weapon seize with dauntless hands,
Entering the cavern; for 'tis fully heated.

CHORUS

Will you not give directions who shall first
Manage the glowing lever, and burn out
The Cyclops' eye, that in one common fortune
We all may share.

SEMICHORUS I.

We who before the portals
Are station'd, are not tall enough to drive
Full on its destin'd mark the hissing brand.

SEMICHORUS II.

But I am with a sudden lameness seiz'd.,

SEMICHORUS I.

The same calamity which you ex fence
To me hath also happen'd; for my feet
Are by convulsions tortur'd, tho' the cause
I know not.

ULYSSES
     If ye feel, such dreadful spasms,
How can ye stand?

CHORUS
        Our eyes are also fill'd
With dust or ashes.

ULYSSES
             These allies of mine   820
        Are worthless cowards.

CHORUS
          We forsooth want courage
Because we feel compassion for our shoulders,
Nor would be beaten till our teeth drop out.
But I a magic incantation know,   825
Devis'd by Orpheus, which hath such effect,
That of its own accord the brand shall pierce
The skull of him, the one-ey'd Son of Earth.

ULYSSES
    Long have-I known ye are by nature such;   830
But more than ever do I know you now.
On my own friends I therefore must rely.
Yet if thou past no vigour in that arm,
Exhort my drooping friends to act with valour
And let thy counsels aid the bold enterprise.   835

                            (Exit ULYSSES.)

CHORUS
     Such be my province: we this Carian's life
Will hazard. But my counsels shall induce them
To burn the Cyclops. Ho! with courage whirl
The brand, delay not to scorch out the eye
Of him who banquets on the stranger's flesh.   840
With fire assail the savage, pierce the front
Of Aetna's shepherd, lest, with anguish stung;
On you he perpetrate some deed of horror.

POLYPHEME
(Within.)
    Ah me! by burning coals I am depriv'd
Of eye-sight.   845

CHORUS
That was a melodious Paean:
To me, O Cyclops, sing th' enchanting strain.

POLYPHEME, CHORUS

POLYPHEME
Ah, bow am I insulted and destroy'd!
Yet shall ye never from this hollow rock
Escape triumphant, O ye things of nought   850
For in my station rooted, where this cleft
Opens a door, will .I spread forth my hands
And stop your passage?

CHORUS
Ha! what means these outcries
O Cyclops?   855

POLYPHEME
I am ruin'd.

CHORUS
You appear
To have much been abus'd.

POLYPHEME
Deplorably.

CHORUS
When fuddled, did you fall 'mid burning colas?   860

POLYPHEME
Noman hath ruin'd me.

CHORUS
To you then no one
Hath offer'd any wrong.

POLYPHEME
These lids hath Noman
Depriv'd of sight.   865

CHORUS
You therefore are not blind.

POLYPHEME
Wouldst thou could'st see as little.

CHORUS
How can no man
Put out your eye.

POLYPHEME
Thou art dispos'd to jest.
But where is Noman?

CHORUS
He is no where, Cyclops.

POLYPHEME
That execrable stranger, mark me well,
Is author of my ruin, who produc'd
The fraudful draught, and burn'd my visual nerves.

CHORUS
Wine is invincible.

POLYPHEME
By all the Gods,
Answer me I conjure you; did they fly,
Or are they here within?

CHORUS
They on the top
Of yonder rock which skreens them from your reach,
In silence take their stand.

POLYPHEME
But on which side?

CHORUS
Your right.

POLYPHEME
Where, where?

CHORUS
Upon that very rock.
Have you yet caught them?

POLYPHEME
To mischance succeeds
Mischance; I have fallen down and crack'd my skull.

CHORUS
They 'scape you now.   890

POLYPHEME
        Ye misinform'd me sure;
They are not here.

CHORUS
        I say not that they are.

POLYPHEME
Where then?

CHORUS
        They wheel around your on your left.   895

POLYPHEME
   Ah me! I am derided, ye but mock
At my affliction.'

CHORUS
        They are there no longer:
But Noman stands before you.

POLYPHEME
                        O thou villain,   900
Where art thou?

ULYSSES, POLYPHEME, CHORUS

ULYSSES
        Keeping cautiously aloof,
Thus I, Ulysses, guard my threaten'd life.

POLYPHEME
   What said'st thou? Wherefore hast thou chang'd thy name
T' assume a new one?   905

ULYSSES
        Me my father nam'd
Ulysses. It was destin'd you should suffer
 A just requital for your impious feast;
For I in vain had with consuming flames
Laid Ilion waste, had I forborn t' avenge   910
On you the murder of my valiant friends.

POLYPHEME
Now is that antient oracle, alas,
Accomplish'd, which foretold, that I by thee,
On thy return from Troy, should be depriv'd
Of sight: but that thou also for a deed
So cruel, shalt be punish'd, and full long
Endure the beating of tempestuous waves.

ULYSSES
Go weep, my actions justify these words.
But to the shore I haste; and to my country
Will steer the vessel o'er Sicilia's waves.

POLYPHEME
Thou shalt not; with this fragment of the rock
Hurl'd at thy head, thee and thy perjur'd crew
Will I demolish: for I yet, tho' blind,
Can mount the cliff which overhangs the port,
And in its wonted crannies fix my steps.

CHORUS
But we, blest partners in Ulysses' voyage,
Henceforth the laws of Bacchus will obey.

(Exit.)

(LIGHTS FADE.)

(CURTAINS.)

(END OF PLAY.)

The Cyclops

Translated by

Edward P. Coleridge

Dramatis Personae

SILENUS

CHORUS OF SATYRS

ODYSSEUS

THE CYCLOPS

SCENE: Mount Aetna in Sicily, before
                               the cave of Cyclops.

SILENUS

O Bromius, unnumbered are the toils I bear because of thee, no less now than when I was young and hale; first, when thou wert driven mad by Hera and didst leave the mountain nymphs, thy nurses; next, when in battle with earth-born spearmen I stood beside thee on the right as squire, and slew Enceladus, smiting him full in the middle of his targe with my spear. Come, though, let me see; must I confess 'twas all a dream? No, by Zeus! since I really showed his spoils to the Bacchic god. And now am I enduring to the full a toil still worse than those. For when Hera sent forth a race of Tyrrhene pirates against thee, that thou mightest be smuggled far away, I, as soon as the news reached me, sailed in quest of thee with my children; and, taking the helm myself, I stood on the end of the stern and steered our trim craft; and my sons, sitting at the oars, made the grey billows froth and foam as they sought thee, my liege, But just as we had come nigh Malea in our course, an east wind blew upon the ship and drove us hither to the rock of Aetna, where in lonely caverns dwell the one-eyed children of ocean's god, the murdering Cyclopes. Captured by one of them we are slaves in his house; Polyphemus they call him whom we serve; and instead of Bacchic revelry we are herding a godless Cyclops's flocks; and so it is my children, striplings as they are, tend the young thereof on the edge of the downs; while my appointed task is to stay here and fill the troughs and sweep out the cave, or wait upon the ungodly Cyclops at his impious feasts. His orders now compel obedience; I have to scrape out his house with the rake you see, so as to receive the Cyclops, my absent master, and his sheep in clean caverns. 28

But already I see my children driving their browsing flocks towards me.

What means this? is the beat of feet in the Sicinnis dance the same to you now as when ye attended the Bacchic god in his revelries and made your way with dainty steps to the music of lyres to the halls of Althaea? 32

CHORUS

Offspring of well-bred sires and dams, pray whither wilt thou be gone from me to the rocks? Hast thou not here a gentle breeze, and grass to browse, and water from the eddying stream set near the cave in troughs? and are not thy young ones bleating for thee? 36

Pst! pst! wilt thou not browse here, here on the dewy slope? Ho! ho ere long will I cast a stone at thee. Away, away! O horned one, to the fold-keeper of the Cyclops, the country-ranging shepherd. Loosen thy bursting udder; welcome to thy teats the kids, whom thou leavest in the lambkins' pens. Those little bleating kids, asleep the livelong day, miss thee; wilt then leave at last the rich grass pastures on the peaks of Aetna and enter the fold? . . .   43

Here we have no Bromian god; no dances here, or Bacchantes thyrsus-bearing; no roll of drums, or drops of sparkling wine by gurgling founts; nor is it now with Nymphs in Nysa I sing a song of Bacchus, Bacchus! to the queen of love, in quest of whom I once sped on with Bacchantes, white of foot.   47

Dear friend, dear Bacchic god, whither art roaming alone, waving thy auburn locks, while I, thy minister, do service to the one-eyed Cyclops, a slave and wanderer I, clad in this wretched goat-skin dress, severed from thy love?   50

                    SILENUS
Hush, children! and bid our servants fold the flocks in the rock-roofed cavern.

                    CHORUS
                 (To SERVANTS.)
Away!

                  (To SILENUS.)
But prithee, why such haste, father?   53

                    SILENUS
I see the hull of a ship from Hellas at the shore, and men, that wield the oar, on their way to this cave with some chieftain. About their necks they carry empty vessels and pitchers for water; they are in want of food. Luckless strangers! who can they be? They know not what manner of man our master Polyphemus is, to have set foot here in his cheerless abode and come to the jaws of the cannibal Cyclops in an evil hour. But hold ye your peace, that we may inquire whence they come to the peak of Sicilian Aetna.   61

                    ODYSSEUS
Pray tell us, sirs, of some river-spring whence we might draw a draught to slake our thirst, or of someone willing to sell victuals to mariners in need.

Why, what is this? We seem to have chanced upon a city of the Bromian god; here by the caves I see a group of Satyrs. To the eldest first I bid "All hail!   65

SILENUS
All hail, sir! tell me who thou art, and name thy country.

ODYSSEUS
Odysseus of Ithaca, king of the Cephallenians' land.

SILENUS
I know him for a prating knave, one of Sisyphus' shrewd offspring.

ODYSSEUS
I am the man; abuse me not.

SILENUS
Whence hast thou sailed hither to Sicily?   70

ODYSSEUS
From Ilium and the toils of Troy.

SILENUS
How was that? didst thou not know the passage to thy native land?

ODYSSEUS
Tempestuous winds drove me hither against my will.

SILENUS
God wot! thou art in the same plight as I am.

ODYSSEUS
Why, wert thou too drifted hither against thy will?   75

SILENUS
I was, as I pursued the pirates who carried Bromius off.

ODYSSEUS
What land is this and who are its inhabitants?

SILENUS
This is mount Aetna, the highest point in Sicily.

ODYSSEUS
But where are the city-walls and ramparts?

SILENUS
There are none; the headlands, sir, are void of men.   80

ODYSSEUS
Who then possess the land? the race of wild creatures?

SILENUS
The Cyclopes, who have caves, not roofed houses.

ODYSSEUS
Obedient unto whom? or is the power in the people's hands?

SILENUS
They are rovers; no man obeys another in anything.

ODYSSEUS
Do they sow Demeter's grain, or on what do they live?   85

SILENUS
On milk and cheese and flesh of sheep.

ODYSSEUS
Have they the drink of Bromius, the juice of the vine?

SILENUS
No indeed! and thus it is a joyless land they dwell in.

ODYSSEUS
Are they hospitable and reverent towards strangers?

SILENUS
Strangers, they say, supply the daintiest meat.   90

ODYSSEUS
What, do they delight in killing men and eating them?

SILENUS
No one has ever arrived here without being butchered.

ODYSSEUS
Where is the Cyclops himself? inside his dwelling?

SILENUS
He is gone hunting wild beasts with hounds on Aetna.

ODYSSEUS
Dost know then what to do, that we may be gone from the
land?   95

SILENUS
Not I, Odysseus; but I would do anything for thee.

ODYSSEUS
Sell us food, of which we are in need.

SILENUS
There is nothing but flesh, as I said.

ODYSSEUS
Well, even that is a pleasant preventive of hunger.

SILENUS
And there is cheese curdled with fig-juice, and the milk
of kine.   100

ODYSSEUS
Bring them out; a man should see his purchases.

SILENUS
But tell me, how much gold wilt thou give me in exchange?

ODYSSEUS
No gold bring I, but Dionysus' drink.

SILENUS
Most welcome words! I have long been wanting that.   104

ODYSSEUS
Yes, it was Maron, the god's son, who gave me a draught.

SILENUS
What! Maron whom once I dandled in these arms?

ODYSSEUS
The son of the Bacchic god, that thou mayst learn more
certainly.

SILENUS
Is it inside the ship, or hast thou it with thee?

ODYSSEUS
This, as thou seest, is the skin that holds it, old sir.

SILENUS
Why, that would not give me so much as a mouthful.   110

ODYSSEUS
This, and twice as much again as will run from the skin.

SILENUS
Fair the rill thou speakest of, delicious to me.

ODYSSEUS
Shall I let thee taste the wine unmixed, to start with?

SILENUS
A reasonable offer; for of a truth a taste invites the purchase.

ODYSSEUS
Well, I haul about a cup as well as the skin.   115

SILENUS
Come, let it gurgle in, that I may revive my memory by a pull at it.

ODYSSEUS
There then!

SILENUS
Ye gods! what a delicious scent it has!

ODYSSEUS
What! didst thou see it?

SILENUS
No, i' faith, but I smell it.   120

ODYSSEUS
Taste it then, that thy approval may not stop at words.

SILENUS
Zounds! Bacchus is inviting me to dance; ha! ha!

ODYSSEUS
Did it not gurgle finely down thy throttle?

SILENUS
Aye that it did, to the ends of my fingers.

ODYSSEUS
Well, we will give thee money besides.   125

SILENUS

Only undo the skin, and never mind the money.

ODYSSEUS

Bring out the cheeses then and lambs.

SILENUS

I will do so, with small thought of any master. For let me
have a single cup of that and I would turn madman, giving in
exchange for it the flocks of every Cyclops and then throwing
myself into the sea from the Leucadian rock, once I have been
well drunk and smoothed out my wrinkled brow. For if a man
rejoice not in his drinking, he is mad; for in drinking it's
possible for this to stand up straight, and then to fondle
breasts, and to caress well tended locks, and there is dancing
withal, and oblivion of woe. Shall not I then purchase so
rare a drink, bidding the senseless Cyclops and his central
eye go hang?   137

(Exit SILENUS.)

CHORUS

Hearken, Odysseus, let us hold some converse with thee.

ODYSSEUS

Well, do so; ours is a meeting of friends.

CHORUS

Did you take Troy and capture the famous Helen?   140

ODYSSEUS

Aye, and we destroyed the whole family of Priam.

CHORUS

After capturing your blooming prize, were all of you in
turn her lovers? for she likes variety in husbands; the
traitress! the sight of a man with embroidered breeches on
his legs and a golden chain about his neck so fluttered her,
that she left Menelaus, her excellent little husband. Would
there had never been a race of women born into the world at
all, unless it were for me alone!   147

SILENUS
(Reappearing with food.)
Lo! I bring you fat food from the flocks, king Odysseus,
the young of bleating sheep and cheeses of curdled milk
without stint. Carry them away with you and begone from the

cave at once, after giving me a drink of merry grape-juice in
exchange.   151

CHORUS
Alack! yonder comes the Cyclops; what shall we do?

ODYSSEUS
Then truly are we lost, old sir! whither must we fly?

SILENUS
Inside this rock, for there ye may conceal yourselves.

ODYSSEUS
Dangerous advice of thine, to run into the net!   155

SILENUS
No danger; there are ways of escape in plenty in the rock.

ODYSSEUS
No, never that; for surely Troy will groan and loudly too,
if we flee from a single man, when I have oft withstood with
my shield a countless host of Phrygians. Nay, if die we must,
we will die a noble death; or, if we live, we will maintain
our old renown at least with credit.   160

CYCLOPS
A light here! hold it up! what is this? what means this
idleness, your Bacchic revelry? Here have we no Dionysus, nor
clash of brass, nor roll of drums. Pray, how is it with my
newly-born lambs in the caves? are they at the teat, running
close to the side of their dams? Is the full amount of milk
for cheeses milked out in baskets of rushes? How now? what
say you? One of ye will soon be shedding tears from the weight
of my club; look up, not down.   167

CHORUS
There! my head is bent back till I see Zeus himself; I
behold both the stars and Orion.

CYCLOPS
Is my breakfast quite ready?

CHORUS
'Tis laid; be thy throat only ready.   170

CYCLOPS
Are, the bowls too full of milk?

CHORUS

Aye, so that thou canst swill off a whole hogshead, so it please thee.

CYCLOPS

Sheep's milk or cows' milk or a mixture of both?

CHORUS

Whichever thou wilt; don't swallow me, that's all.

CYCLOPS

Not I; for you would start kicking in the pit of my stomach and kill me by your antics.   175
            (Catching sight of ODYSSEUS and his
            followers.)
Ha! what is this crowd I see near the folds? Some pirates or robbers have put in here. Yes, I really see the lambs from my caves tied up there with twisted osiers, cheese-presses scattered about, and old Silenus with his bald pate all swollen with blows.   179

SILENUS

Oh! oh! poor wretch that I am, pounded to a fever.

CYCLOPS

By whom? who has been pounding thy head, old sirrah?

SILENUS

These are the culprits, Cyclops, all because I refused to let them plunder thee.

CYCLOPS

Did they not know I was a god and sprung from gods?   183

SILENUS

That was what I told them, but they persisted in plundering thy goods, and, in spite of my efforts, they actually began to eat the cheese and carry off the lambs; and they said they would tie thee in a three-cubit pillory and tear out thy bowels by force at thy navel, and flay thy back thoroughly with the scourge; and then, after binding thee, fling thy carcase down among the benches of their ship to sell to someone for heaving up stones, or else throw thee into a mill.

CYCLOPS

Oh, indeed! Be off then and sharpen my cleavers at once; heap high the faggots and light them; for they shall be slain

forthwith and fill this maw of mine, what time I pick my feast
hot from the coals, waiting not for carvers, and fish up the
rest from the cauldron boiled and sodden; for I have had my
fill of mountain-fare and sated myself with banquets of lions
and stags, but 'tis long I have been without human flesh.

SILENUS

Truly, master, a change like this is all the sweeter after
everyday fare; for just of late there have been no fresh
arrivals of strangers at these caves.   200

ODYSSEUS

Hear the strangers too in turn, Cyclops. We had come near
the cave from our ship, wishing to procure provisions by
purchase, when this fellow sold us the lambs and handed them
over for a stoup of wine to drink himself, a voluntary act on
both sides, there was no violence employed at all. No, there
is not a particle of truth in the story he tells; now that he
has been caught selling thy property behind thy back.   206

SILENUS

I? Perdition catch thee!

ODYSSEUS

If I am lying, yes.

SILENUS

O Cyclops, by thy sire Poseidon, by mighty Triton and
Nereus, by Calypso and the daughters of Nereus, by the sacred
billows and all the race of fishes! I swear to thee, most
noble sir, dear little Cyclops, master mine, it is not I who
sell thy goods to strangers, else may these children, dearly
as I love them, come to an evil end.   213

CHORUS

Keep that for thyself; with my own eyes I saw thee sell
the goods to the strangers; and if I lie, perdition catch my
sire! but injure not the strangers.

CYCLOPS

Ye lie; for my part I put more faith in him than
Rhadamanthus, declaring him more just. But I have some
questions to ask. Whence sailed ye, strangers? of what country
are you? what city was it nursed your childhood?   218

ODYSSEUS

We are Ithacans by birth, and have been driven from our course by the winds of the sea on our way from Ilium, after sacking its citadel.

CYCLOPS

Are ye the men who visited on Ilium, that bordereth on Scamander's wave, the rape of Helen, worst of women?

ODYSSEUS

We are; that was the fearful labour we endured.

CYCLOPS

A sorry expedition yours, to have sailed to the land of Phrygia for the sake of one woman   223

ODYSSEUS

It was a god's doing; blame not any son of man. But thee do we implore, most noble son of Ocean's god, speaking as free-born men; be not so cruel as to slay thy friends on their coming to thy cave, nor regard us as food for thy jaws, an impious meal; for we preserved thy sire, O king, in possession of his temple-seats deep in the nooks of Hellas; and the sacred port of Taenarus and Malea's furthest coves remain unharmed; and Sunium's rock, the silver-veined, sacred to Zeus-born Athena, still is safe, and Geraestus, the harbour of refuge; and we did not permit Phrygians to put such an intolerable reproach on Hellas. Now in these things thou too hast a share, for thou dwellest in a corner of the land of Hellas beneath Aetna's fire-streaming rock; and although thou turn from arguments, still it is a custom amongst mortal men to receive shipwrecked sailors as their suppliants and show them hospitality and help them with raiment; not that these should fill thy jaws and belly, their limbs transfixed with spits for piercing ox-flesh. The land of Priam hath emptied Hellas quite enough, drinking the blood of many whom the spear laid low, with the ruin it has brought on widowed wives, on aged childless dames, and hoary-headed sires; and if thou roast and consume the remnant,-a meal thou wilt rue,-why, where shall one turn? Nay, be persuaded by me, Cyclops; forego thy ravenous greed and choose piety rather than wickedness; for on many a man ere now unrighteous gains have brought down retribution.   248

SILENUS
. . . I will give thee a word of advice! as for his flesh,
leave not a morsel of it, and if thou eat his tongue, Cyclops,
thou wilt become a monstrous clever talker.   250

CYCLOPS
Wealth, manikin, is the god for the wise; all else is mere
vaunting and fine words. Plague take the headlands by the
sea, on which my father seats himself! Why hast thou put
forward these arguments? I shudder not at Zeus's thunder, nor
know I wherein Zeus is a mightier god than I, stranger; what
is more, I reck not of him; my reasons hear. When he pours
down the rain from above, here in this rock in quarters snug,
feasting on roast calf's flesh or some wild game and
moistening well my up-turned paunch with deep draughts from
a tub of milk, I rival the thunder-claps of Zeus with my
artillery; and when the north wind blows from Thrace and
sheddeth snow, I wrap my carcase in the hides of beasts and
light a fire, and what care I for snow? The earth perforce,
whether she like it or not, produces grass and fattens my
flocks, which I sacrifice to no one save myself and this
belly, the greatest of deities; but to the gods, not I! For
surely to eat and drink one's fill from day to day and give
oneself no grief at all, this is the king of gods for your
wise man, but lawgivers go hang, chequering, as they do, the
life of man! And so I will not cease from indulging myself by
devouring thee; and thou shalt receive this stranger's gift,
that I may be free of blame,-fire and my father's element
yonder, and a cauldron to hold thy flesh and boil it nicely
in collops. So in with you, that ye may feast me well,
standing round the altar to honour the cavern's god.   274

(Enters his cave.)

ODYSSEUS
Alas! escaped from the troubles of Troy and the sea, my
barque now strands upon the whim and forbidding heart of this
savage.
O Pallas, mistress mine, goddess-daughter of Zeus, help
me, help me now; for I am come to toils and depths of peril
worse than all at Ilium; and thou, O Zeus, the stranger's
god, who hast thy dwelling 'mid the radiant stars, behold
these things; for, if thou regard them not, in vain art thou
esteemed the great god Zeus, though but a thing of naught.

(Follows the CYCLOPS reluctantly.)

CHORUS

Ope wide the portal of thy gaping throat, Cyclops; for strangers' limbs, both boiled and grilled, are ready from off the coals for the to gnaw and tear and mince up small, reclining in thy shaggy goat-skin coat.   285

Relinquish not thy meal for me; keep that boat for thyself alone. Avaunt this cave! avaunt the burnt-offerings, which the godless Cyclops offers on Aetna's altars, exulting in meals on strangers' flesh!

Oh! the ruthless monster! to sacrifice his guests at his own hearth, the suppliants of his halls, cleaving and tearing and serving up to his loathsome teeth a feast of human flesh, hot from the coals.   291

ODYSSEUS
(Reappearing with a look of horror.)
O Zeus! what can I say after the hideous sights I have seen inside the cave, things past belief, resembling more the tales men tell than aught they do?

CHORUS

What news, Odysseus? has the Cyclops, most godless monster, been feasting on thy dear comrades?   294

ODYSSEUS

Aye, he singled out a pair, on whom the flesh was fattest and in best condition, and took them up in his hand to weigh.

CHORUS

How went it with you then, poor wretch?   297

ODYSSEUS

When we had entered yonder rocky abode, he lighted first a fire, throwing logs of towering oak upon his spacious hearth, enough for three wagons to carry as their load; next, close by the blazing flame, he placed his couch of pine-boughs laid upon the floor, and filled a bowl of some ten firkins, pouring white milk thereinto, after he had milked his kine; and by his side he put a can of ivy-wood, whose breadth was three cubits and its depth four maybe; next he set his brazen pot a-boiling on the fire, spits too he set beside him, fashioned of the branches of thorn, their points hardened in the fire and the rest of them trimmed with the hatchet, and the blood-bowls of Aetna for the axe's edge. Now when that hell-cook, god-detested, had everything quite ready, he caught up a pair of my companions and proceeded deliberately to cut the throat of one of them over the yawning brazen pot; but the other he clutched by the tendon of his heel, and, striking him against a sharp point of rocky stone, dashed out his brains; then, after hacking the fleshy parts with glutton cleaver, he set to grilling them, but the limbs he threw into his cauldron to seethe. And I, poor wretch, drew near with streaming eyes and waited on the Cyclops; but the others kept cowering like frightened birds in crannies of the rock, and the blood forsook their skin. Anon, when he had gorged himself upon my comrades' flesh and had fallen on his back, breathing heavily, there came a sudden inspiration to me. I filled a cup of this Maronian wine and offered him a draught, saying, "Cyclops, son of Ocean's god, see here what heavenly drink the grapes of Hellas yield, glad gift of Dionysus." He, glutted with his shameless meal, took and drained it at one draught, and, lifting up his hand, he thanked me thus "Dearest to me of all my guests! fair the drink thou givest me to crown so fair a feast." Now when I saw his delight, I gave him another cup, knowing the wine would make him rue it, and he would soon be paying the penalty. Then he set to singing; but I kept filling bumper after bumper and heating him with drink. So there he is singing discordantly amid the weeping of my fellow-sailors, and the cave re-echoes; but I have made my way out quietly and would fain save thee and myself, if thou wilt. Tell me then, is it your wish, or is it not, to fly from this unsocial wretch and take up your abode with Naiad nymphs in the halls of the Bacchic god? Thy father within approves this scheme; but there! he is powerless, getting all he can out of his liquor; his wings are snared by the cup as if he had flown against bird-lime, and he is fuddled; but thou art young and lusty; so save thyself with my help and regain thy old friend Dionysus, so little like the Cyclops. 342

CHORUS

Best of friends, would we might see that day, escaping the godless Cyclops!

ODYSSEUS

Hear then how I will requite this vile monster and rescue you from thraldom.

CHORUS

Tell me how; no note of Asiatic lyre would sound more sweetly in our ears than news of the Cyclops' death. 345

ODYSSEUS

Delighted with this liquor of the Bacchic god, he fain would go a-reveling with his brethren.

CHORUS
I understand; thy purpose is to seize and slay him in the
thickets when clone, or push him down a precipice.

ODYSSEUS
Not at all; my plan is fraught with subtlety.   348

CHORUS
What then? Truly we have long heard of thy cleverness.

ODYSSEUS
I mean to keep him from this revel, saying he must not give
this drink to his brethren but keep it for himself alone and
lead a happy life. Then when he falls asleep, o'ermastered by
the Bacchic god, I will put a point with this sword of mine
to an olive-branch I saw lying in the cave, and will set it
on fire; and when I see it well alight, I will lift the heated
brand, and, thrusting it full in the Cyclops' eye, melt out
his sight with its blaze; and, as when a man in fitting the
timbers of a ship makes his auger spin to and fro with a
double strap, so will I make the brand revolve in the eye,
that gives the Cyclops light and will scorch up the pupil
thereof.   360

CHORUS
Ho! ho! how glad I feel! wild with joy at the contrivance!

ODYSSEUS
That done, I will embark thee and those thou lovest with
old Silenus in the deep hold of my black ship, my ship with
double banks of oars, and carry you away from this land.

CHORUS
Well, can I too lay hold of the blinding brand, as though
the god's libation had been poured? for I would fain have a
share in this offering of blood.   365

ODYSSEUS
Indeed thou must, for the brand is large, and thou must
help hold it.

CHORUS
How lightly would I lift the load of e'en a hundred wains,
if that will help us to grub out the eye of the doomed Cyclops,
like a wasp's nest.   368

ODYSSEUS

Hush! for now thou knowest my plot in full, and when I bid you, obey the author of it; for I am not the man to desert my friends inside the cave and save myself alone. And yet I might escape; I am clear of the cavern's depths already; but no! to desert the friends with whom I journeyed hither and only save myself is not a righteous course.   373

(R-enters the cave.)

FIRST HALF-CHORUS

Come, who will be the first and who the next to him upon the list to grip the handle of the brand, and, thrusting it into the Cyclops' eye, gouge out the light thereof?

SECOND HALF-CHORUS

Hush! hush! Behold the drunkard leaves his rocky home, trolling loud some hideous lay, a clumsy tuneless clown, whom tears await. Come, let us give this boor a lesson in revelry. Ere long will he be blind at any rate.   378

FIRST HALF-CHORUS

Happy he who plays the Bacchanal amid the precious streams distilled from grapes, stretched at full length for a revel, his arm around the friend he loves, and some fair dainty damsel on his couch, his hair perfumed with nard and glossy, the while he calls, "Oh! who will ope the door for me?"

CYCLOPS

Ha! ha! full of wine and merry with a feast's good cheer am I, my hold freighted like a merchant-ship up to my belly's very top. This turf graciously invites me to seek my brother Cyclopes for revel in the spring-tide.   385
Come, stranger, bring the wine-skin hither and hand it over to me.

SECOND HALF-CHORUS

Forth from the house its fair lord comes, casting his fair glance round him. We have someone to befriend us. A hostile brand is awaiting thee, no tender bride in dewy grot. No single colour will those garlands have, that soon shall cling so close about thy brow.   390

ODYSSEUS
(Returning with the wine-skin.)
Hearken, Cyclops; for I am well versed in the ways of Bacchus, whom I have given thee to drink.

CYCLOPS
And who is Bacchus? some reputed god?

ODYSSEUS
The greatest god men know to cheer their life.

CYCLOPS
I like his after-taste at any rate.   395

ODYSSEUS
This is the kind of god he is; he harmeth no man.

CYCLOPS
But how does a god like being housed in a wine-skin?

ODYSSEUS
Put him where one may, he is content there.

CYCLOPS
It is not right that gods should be clad in leather.

ODYSSEUS
What of that, provided he please thee? does the leather
hurt thee?   400

CYCLOPS
I hate the wine-skin, but the liquor we have here I love.

ODYSSEUS
Stay, then, Cyclops; drink and be merry.

CYCLOPS
Must I not give my brethren a share in this liquor?

ODYSSEUS
No, keep it thyself and thou wilt appear of more honour.

CYCLOPS
Give it my friends and I shall appear of more use.   405

ODYSSEUS
Revelling is apt to end in blows, abuse, and strife.

CYCLOPS
I may be drunk, but no man will lay hands on me for all
that.

ODYSSEUS
Better stay at home, my friend, after a carouse.

CYCLOPS
Who loves not revelling then is but a simpleton.

ODYSSEUS
But whoso stays at home, when drunk, is wise.   410

CYCLOPS
What shall we do, Silenus? art minded to stay?

SILENUS
That I am; for what need have we of others to share our drink, Cyclops?

CYCLOPS
Well, truly the turf is soft as down with its fresh flowering plants.

SILENUS
(Seating himself.)
Aye, and 'tis pleasant drinking in the warm sunshine.

CYLOPS
. . .

SILENUS
Come, let me see thee stretch thy carcase on the ground.

CYCLOPS
(Sitting down.)
(There then!) Why art thou putting the mixing-bowl behind me?   416

SILENUS
That no one passing by may upset it.

CYCLOPS
Nay, but thy purpose is to drink upon the sly; set it between us.
(To ODYSSEUS.)
Now tell me, stranger, by what name to call thee.

ODYSSEUS
Noman. What boon shall I receive of thee to earn my thanks?

CYCLOPS

I will feast on thee last, after all thy comrades.   421

ODYSSEUS

Fair indeed the honour thou bestowest on thy guest, sir Cyclops!

CYCLOPS
(Turning suddenly to SILENUS.)
Ho, sirrah! what art thou about? taking a stealthy pull at the wine?

SILENUS

No, but it kissed me for my good looks.

CYCLOPS

Thou shalt smart, if thou kiss the wine when it kisses not thee.   425

SILENUS

Oh! but it did, for it says it is in love with my handsome face.

CYCLOPS
(Holding out his cup.)
Pour in; only give me my cup full.

SILENUS

H'm! how is it mixed? just let me make sure.

(Takes another pull.)

CYCLOPS

Perdition! give it me at once.

SILENUS

Oh, no! I really cannot, till I see thee with a crown on, and have another taste myself.   430

CYCLOPS

My cup-bearer is a cheat.

SILENUS

No really, but the wine is so luscious. Thou must wipe thy lips, though, to get a draught.

CYCLOPS
There! my lips and beard are clean now.

SILENUS
Bend thine elbow gracefully, and then quaff thy cup, as
thou seest me do, and as now thou seest me not.   435

(Burying his face in his cup.)

CYCLOPS
Aha! what next?

SILENUS
I drunk it off at a draught with much pleasure.

CYCLOPS
Stranger, take the skin thyself and be my cup-bearer.

ODYSSEUS
Well, at any rate the grape is no stranger to my hand.

CYCLOPS
Come, pour it in.   440

ODYSSEUS
In it goes! keep silence, that is all.

CYCLOPS
A difficult task when a man is deep in his cups.

ODYSSEUS
Here, take and drink it off; leave none.

CLYCLOPS
. . .

ODYSSEUS
Thou must be silent and only give in when the liquor does.

CYCLOPS
God wot! it is a clever stock that bears the grape.   445

ODYSSEUS
Aye, and if thou but swallow plenty of it after a plentiful
meal, moistening thy belly till its thirst is gone, it will
throw thee into slumber; but if thou leave aught behind, the
Bacchic god will parch thee for it.   448

CYCLOPS

Ha! ha! what a trouble it was getting out! This is pleasure unalloyed; earth and sky seem whirling round together; I see the throne of Zeus and all the godhead's majesty. Kiss *thee*! no! There are the Graces trying to tempt me. I shall rest well enough with my Ganymede here; yea, by the Graces, right fairly; for I like lads better than the wenches.   453

SILENUS

What! Cyclops, am I Ganymede, Zeus's minion?

CYCLOPS
                (Attempting to carry him into the
                cave.)
To be sure, Ganymede whom I am carrying off from the halls of Dardanus.

SILENUS

I am undone, my children; outrageous treatment waits me.

CHORUS

Dost find fault with thy lover? dost scorn him in his cups?

SILENUS

Woe is me! most bitter shall I find the wine ere long. 458

                        (Exit SILENUS,
                        dragged away by
                        CYCLOPS.)

ODYSSEUS

Up now, children of Dionysus, sons of a noble sire, soon will yon creature in the cave, relaxed in slumber as ye see him, spew from his shameless maw the meat. Already the brand inside his lair is vomiting cloud of smoke; and the only reason we prepared it was to burn the Cyclops' eye; so mind thou quit thee like a man.   463

CHORUS

I will have a spirit as of rock or adamant; but go inside, before my father suffers any shameful treatment; for here thou hast things ready.

ODYSSEUS

O Hephaestus, lord of Aetna, rid thyself for once and all of a troublesome neighbour by burning his bright eye out. Come, Sleep, as well, offspring of sable Night, come with all thy power on the monster god-detested; and never after Troy's most glorious toils destroy Odysseus and his crew by the hands of one who recketh naught of God or man; else roust we reckon Chance a goddess, and Heaven's will inferior to hers.   471

(ODYSSEUS re-enters the cave.)

CHORUS
Tightly the pincers shall grip the neck of him who feasts upon his guests; for soon will he lose the light of his eye by fire; already the brand, a tree's huge limb, lurks amid the embers charred.   474
Oh! come ye then and work his doom, pluck out the maddened Cyclops' eye, that he may rue his drinking. And I too fain would leave the Cyclops' lonely land and see king Bromius, ivy-crowned, the god I sorely miss. Ah! shall I ever come to that?   477

ODYSSEUS
(Leaving the cave cautiously.)
Silence, ye cattle! I adjure you; close your lips; make not a sound I'll not let a man of you so much as breathe or wink or clear his throat, that yon pest awake not, until the sight in the Cyclops' eye has passed through the fiery ordeal.

CHORUS
Silent we stand with 'bated breath.   481

ODYSSEUS
In then, and mind your fingers grip the brand, for it is splendidly red-hot.

CHORUS
Thyself ordain who first must seize the blazing bar and burn the Cyclops' eye out, that we may share alike whate'er betides.

FIRST HALF-CHORUS
Standing where I am before the door, I am too far off to thrust the fire into his eye.   485

SECOND HALF-CHORUS
I have just gone lame.

FIRST HALF-CHORUS

Why, then, thou art in the same plight as I; for somehow
or other I sprained my ankle, standing still.

ODYSSEUS

Sprained thy ankle, standing still?

SECOND HALF-CHORUS

Yes, and my eyes are full of dust or ashes from somewhere
or other.

ODYSSEUS

These are sorry fellows, worthless as allies.   490

CHORUS

Because I feel for my back and spine, and express no wish
to have my teeth knocked out, I am a coward, am I? Well, but
I know a spell of Orpheus, a most excellent one, to make the
brand enter his skull of its own accord, and set alight the
one-eyed son of Earth.   493

ODYSSEUS

Long since I knew thou wert by nature such an one, and now
I know it better; I must employ my own friends; but, though
thou bring no active aid, cheer us on at any rate, that I may
find my friends emboldened by thy encouragement.   495

(Exit ODYSSEUS.)

CHORUS

That will I do; the Carian shall run the risk for us; and
as far as encouragement goes, let the Cyclops smoulder.
What ho! my gallants, thrust away, make haste and burn his
eyebrow off, the monster's guest-devouring. Oh! singe and
scorch the shepherd of Aetna; twirl the brand and drag it
round and be careful lest in his agony he treat thee to some
wantonness.   501

CYCLOPS
(Bellowing in the cave.)
Oh! oh! my once bright eye is burnt to cinders now.

CHORUS
Sweet indeed the triumph-song; pray sing it to us, Cyclops.

CYCLOPS
(From within.)
Oh! oh! once more; what outrage on me and what ruin! But never shall ye escape this rocky cave unpunished, ye worthless creatures; for will stand in the entrance of the cleft and fit my hands into it thus.   506

(Staggering to the entrance.)

CHORUS
Why dost thou cry out, Cyclops?

CYCLOPS
I am undone.

CHORUS
Thou art indeed a sorry sight.

CYCLOPS
Aye, and a sad one, too.   510

CHORUS
Didst fall among the coals in a drunken fit?

CYCLOPS
Noman has undone me,

CHORUS
Then there is no one hurting thee after all.

CYCLOPS
Noman is blinding me.

CHORUS
Then art thou not blind.   515

CYCLOPS
As blind as thou, forsooth.

CHORUS
How, pray, could no man have made thee blind?

CYCLOPS
Thou mockest me; but where is this Noman?

CHORUS
Nowhere, Cyclops.

CYCLOPS

It was the stranger, vile wretch! who proved my ruin, that
thou mayst understand rightly, by swilling me with the liquor
he gave me.   521

CHORUS

Ah! wine is a terrible foe, hard to wrestle with.

CYCLOPS

Tell me, I adjure thee, have they escaped or are they still
within?

CHORUS

Here they are ranged in silence, taking the rock to screen
them.

CYCLOPS

On which side?   525

CHORUS

On thy right.

CYCLOPS

Where?

CHORUS

Close against the rock. Hast caught them?

CYCLOPS

Trouble on trouble! I have run my skull against the rock
and cracked it

CHORUS

Aye, and they are escaping thee.   530

CYCLOPS

This way, was it not? 'Twas this way thou saidst.

CHORUS

No, not this way.

CYCLOPS

Which then?

CHORUS

They are getting round thee on the left.   534

CYCLOPS

Alas! I am being mocked; ye jeer me in my evil plight.

CHORUS

They are no longer there; but facing thee that stranger
stands.

CYCLOPS

Master of villainy, where, oh! where art thou?

ODYSSEUS

Some way from thee I am keeping careful guard over the
person of Odysseus.

CYCLOPS

What, a new name! hast changed thine?   539

ODYSSEUS

Yes, Odysseus, the name my father gave me. But thou wert
doomed to pay for thy unholy feast; for I should have seen
Troy burned to but sorry purpose, unless I had avenged on
thee the slaughter of my comrades.   542

CYCLOPS

Woe is me! 'tis an old oracle coming true; yes, it said I
should have my eye put out by thee on thy way home from Troy;
but it likewise foretold that thou wouldst surely pay for
this, tossing on the sea for many day.   545

ODYSSEUS

Go hang! E'en as I say, so have I done. And now will I get
me to the beach and start my hollow ship across the sea of
Sicily to the land of my fathers.

CYCLOPS

Thou shalt not; I will break a boulder off this rock and
crush thee, crew and all, beneath my throw. Blind though I
be, I will climb the hill, mounting through yonder tunnel.

CHORUS

As for us, henceforth will we be the servants of Bacchus,
sharing the voyage of this hero Odysseus.   551

(Exit.)

(LIGHTS FADE.)

(CURTAINS.)

(END OF PLAY.)

CYCLOPS

Translated by

Arthur S. Way

DRAMATIS PERSONAE

SILENUS:	An old attendant of Bacchus
ODYSSEUS:	King of Ithaca.
CYCLOPS:	A one-eyed giant.
CHORUS:	Consisting of Satyrs.

Men of Odysseus' crew.

SCENE: At the entrance to a great
                                cave at the foot of Mount
                                Etna.

AT RISE: Enter from the cave SILENUS,
                                dragging after him a rusty
                                iron rake.

                          SILENUS
O Bacchus!—oh the back-aches that I got
In your cause, when my youthful blood was hot:
First, when, with addled brains through Hera's curses,
You bolted from the Mountain-maids, your nurses;
Next time, when, in the Battle o' Phlegra Field,   5
I was your right-hand man, and through the shield
Of Giant Whatshisname I neatly put
A yard of spear— what, dreamed all this? Tut, tut!
Did Bacchus dream I showed the monster's spoils
To him? Ah, that was play beside these toils!   10
For, O my Bacchus, Hera set on you
A gang of thieves, a Tuscan pirate-crew,
To take you on a very distant trip.
I heard of it, and promptly manned a ship
with my wild boys, and sailed upon the quest.   15
I took the helm, and—well, I did my best;
And the boys rowed—at least, made shift to fling
Some foam about; and so we sought our king.
But, just as on our quarter Malea lay.
An east wind blew, and cast our ship away   20
Upon this rocky shore by Etna's roots,
Home of the Cyclops (Neptune's amours' fruits).
One-eyed, cave-kennelled, man-devouring brutes.
One of them caught us, so that we became
Slaves in his den; and this slave-driver's name   25
Is Polyphemus. No more Bacchanal song
And dance for us! We've got to herd a throng
Of this ungodly villain's goats and sheep:
Yes, my poor boys on far-off hill-sides steep—
My tender ones—are tending flocks for him!   30
And I'm a prisoner here, must fill to the brim
His sheep-troughs: I must sweep this stinking den
For godless Goggle-eye, must turn cook then,
And serve his cursed dinners up—fried men!
Now with this clumsiest of iron rakes   35
                 (Kicks it.)
I must needs clear up all the mess *he* makes.

To welcome home my lord, old Saucer-eye,
And his sheep with him, into a clean—sty.
Ah, here my boys come, driving home the bleating
Flocks; yes, I see them what, is that the beating   40
Of dancing feet? It's like old times, when round
Althaea's house, with Bacchus, to the sound
Of song and harp, your toes scarce touched the ground.

                              (Enter CHORUS,
                              driving goals and
                              sheep.)

                    A SATYR
                (To a he-goat.)
O come along, Sir Billy! If your father *was* a king.
And your mother queen of Nannies, still you needn't
      go and spring   45
Over cliff and crag up yonder: it's good enough for you
Down here, where winds are sleeping, and where
        green as ever grew
        Is the grass that waits the cropping;
        And the rippling water, slopping
Out of all the troughs full-brimming by the cave, is
      full in view;
        And your little kids are pleading   50
        "Come you down!"—and never heeding
From the steep you still are hanging, all bedraggled
      with the dew.
Here goes a stone to stir you! Shoo, you wilful rascal.
      Shoo!
Come you down, and come this minute, you nasty
      horned thing!
Don't you hear your keeper calling, farmer Giant's
      underling?   55

                  ANOTHER SATYR
                (To a she-goat.)
Come, my pretty, to the milking; then away you
      skip, to meet
Your little babies, hungry to nose the heavy teat;
For you left them at the dawning, on the rushes
      where they lay,
And they sorely need refreshment, after sleeping
      all the day.
        Don't you see your little sweeting?   60
        Can't you hear his hungry bleating?
O leave the grassy pasture, to the folding come away!

> Enter here, your cave is ready
> Under Etna, clean and shady:—
O dear! no sign of Bacchus nor his Bacchanal array!
There's no clashing of the cymbals, no dances reel
  and sway,
Nothing trickling from a wine-jar in droppings honey-sweet.
Nor beside the gushing fountains trip the Mountain-
  maidens' feet.

CHORUS OF ALL THE SATYRS

O Aphrodite! and O the mighty
Spell of the chant that thrilled the air,
When to its cadence I chased the maidens.
The Bacchanal girls, and the feet snow-fair!
O Bacchus, only-beloved, all lonely
Now, you are wandering where, ah where,
Of me unbeholden, tossing the golden
Nectar-breathing cloud of your hair?
And I, your vassal, a slave in the castle-
Dungeon of one-eyed Giant Despair,
A slave sheep-drover, with naught to cover
My limbs but a foul goat's skin worn bare,
I wander, breaking my heart with aching
For my lost love far from the voice of my prayer.

SILENUS

Hush, boys! Quick, tell the lads to get the flock
In haste beneath the cavern's roof of rock.

CHORUS

Look sharp there! Where's the hurry, father, now?

SILENUS

Down on the beach I spy a Greek ship's prow;
I see the kings o' the oar—their captain's there—
Come tramping towards this cave. Aha, they bear
Slung round their necks some baskets. Come to beg
For food, of course—and water; there's the keg.
O you poor wretches! Who on earth are these?
Little they dream what hospitalities
Are by the master of this house bestowed,
Who tread this strangely hospitable road
Up to the doors of—Goggle-eyes's jaw.
For right warm welcome to his cannibal maw!
Now we shall learn—if you will just keep still—
Whence come these to Sicilian Etna's hill.

                                    (Enter ODYSSEUS and
                                    crew.)

                    ODYSSEUS
Friends, can you tell us whereabouts to find
Some running water? If you'd be so kind,   100
Moreover as to sell us hungry tars
Something to eat—but what, what? O my stars!
Is this the City of Bacchus that we've found?
Here's quite a crowd of Satyrs standing round
A cave! A fatherly old party, too,   105
A patriarch quite—good morning, Sir, to you!

                    SILENUS
Good morning. What's your name and whence d'you come?

                    ODYSSEUS
Odysseus—Isle-king—Ithaca's my home.

                    SILENUS
Ah, Sisyphus' son! Sharp rogue, a sight too clever!

                    ODYSSEUS
That's me. You needn't call hard names, however.   110

                    SILENUS
And whence do you come to Sicily, may I ask?

                    ODYSSEUS
From taking Troy—tough job, a ten years' task.

                    SILENUS
What, didn't you know the way back to your door?

                    ODYSSEUS
A hurricane caught us, cast us on this shore

                    SILENUS
Heavens! You and I are in one boat together!   115

                    ODYSSEUS
What? you too driven here by stress of weather?

                    SILENUS
Pirates had kidnapped Bacchus: we gave chase.

ODYSSEUS
H'm— what's the land called? Who live in this place?

SILENUS
That's Etna—highest point of Sicily.

ODYSSEUS
But—where's the city? Never a tower I see.

SILENUS
There's none, nor any men—waste hills and lonely.

ODYSSEUS
What, no inhabitants?—the wild beasts only?

SILENUS
Cyclops—no houses—burrow in caves, like rats.

ODYSSEUS
Who is their king?—or are they democrats?

SILENUS
Shepherds—and not for nobody they don't care.

ODYSSEUS
Do they sow corn?—or what's their daily fare?

SILENUS
Milk, cheese—and the eternal mutton-chop.

ODYSSEUS
Do they grow vines, make wine?
                (Sees Silenus' expression.)
What, never a drop?

SILENUS
                (With bitter emphasis.)
Not—one—least—drop! No songs or dances here!

ODYSSEUS
Hospitable? Do strangers get good cheer?

SILENUS
Their special dainty is—the flesh of strangers!

ODYSSEUS
What, what?—they're cannibals, these desert-rangers?

SILENUS
So far, they've butchered every man who's come.

ODYSSEUS
And where's this Cyclops?—don't say he's at home!   135

SILENUS
No, gone to Etna with his hounds to-day.

ODYSSEUS
Do something for us: then we'll get away.

SILENUS
What is it?
                    (Unctuously.)
I'd do anything for you.

ODYSSEUS
Sell us some food. They're famished, are my crew.   140

SILENUS
There's nothing, as I said, save only meat.

ODYSSEUS
Tough mutton.—h'm; well, starving men must eat.

SILENUS
Cream-cheeses too, and milk—a very sea.

ODYSSEUS
Let's see 'em first—no pig-in-a-poke for me!

SILENUS
You show your money—pay before you dine!   145

ODYSSEUS
Better than money: what I've got here—wine!

SILENUS
Wine? Blessed word—last tasted long agone!

ODYSSEUS
'Twas Maron gave it me, your Wine-god's son.

SILENUS
Dear boy!—these arms have nursed you, and here I
    find you!

ODYSSEUS
Yes, Bacchus' best brew, from his own son, mind you.   150

SILENUS
Got the wine with you?—*not* in yon ship's hold?

ODYSSEUS
Old man, it's in this very skin—behold!

(Shows corner of skin.)

SILENUS
That!—why there's not a toothful in't, I swear.

ODYSSEUS
There's twice as much as you can hold in there.

(Shows whole skin.)

SILENUS
Oh—h! what a fountain of delight! O sweet!   155

ODYSSEUS
Have a small taste? No water in it—neat.

SILENUS
Right! "Wet a bargain with a glass," you know.

ODYSSEUS
Here then:—his skinship's got his boat in tow.

(Shows cup hanging from wine-
skin.)

SILENUS
Quick! Trot him out: revive my memory.
I've clean forgot the taste of it.   160

ODYSSEUS
(Pouring.)
There—see?

SILENUS
Oh—oh! I say! What a bouquet!—divine!

ODYSSEUS
Bouquet?—d'ye see one?

SILENUS

No; this nose of mine.
By Jove, can answer for it right enough.   165

ODYSSEUS

Try if it's worth your praise—just taste the stuff.

SILENUS

(Drinks.)
Oh! oh! I *must* dance! Bacchus sounds the note!

ODYSSEUS

Did it slip very sweetly down your throat?

SILENUS

Throat, man?—to my very toes! I feel 'em tingling.

ODYSSEUS

I'll pay cash too: I've got it ready-jingling.   170

SILENUS

Wine! wine!—for money I don't care a button.

ODYSSEUS

All right. Fetch out your cheeses and your mutton.

SILENUS

I will! For master I don't care one fig!
So mad I am for just another swig,
That I'd sell for it all the giants' flocks—   175
Ay, chuck them in the sea from yonder rocks.
If once I get well drunk, and smooth my brow
Clear of the wrinkles drawn by trouble's plough.
The man that isn't jolly after drinking
Is just a drivelling idiot, to my thinking.   180
Jolly's no word for it!—I see a vision
Of snowy bosoms, of delights Elysian;
Of fingers fondling silken hair, of dancing,
Oblivion of all care!—O dream entrancing!
And shall my lips not kiss the cup whence come   185
Such raptures? And shall I not snap my thumb
At Goggle-eye, the blockhead, and the horrid
One eye stuck in the middle of his forehead.

(Goes off to
collect the goods.)

SATYR
Look here, Odysseus; let me ask some questions.

ODYSSEUS
Of course: from friends I welcome all suggestions.   190

SATYR
Did you take Troy, and capture Helen too?

ODYSSEUS
O yes: all Priam's house we overthrew.

SATYR
Well, when you'd caught the naughty little jade,
Didn't each man whip out his vorpal blade,
And thrust her through, one after another, then.   195
And let her have for once her fill of men!
The baggage!—fell in love, all in a twinkle,
with Paris's gaudy bags, without a wrinkle
Fitted to his fine legs, and lost her heart
To his gold necklace! And she must depart,   200
And leave the best of little chaps all lonely,
Menelaus! 'Tell you what it is—if only
No woman lived, a good thing would it be—
Not one on earth—except a few for me.

(Enter SILENUS with
SATYRS bringing
bowls and lambs.)

SILENUS
Here, king Odysseus, here they come, the lambs,   205
Warranted tender babes of bleating dams;
Here are the curds, and cheeses too galore.
Catch hold, and hurry 'em down from cave to shore.
Now for the grape's pure soul, for Bacchus' brew!—
O lor!—the Cyclops! Oh, what shall we do?   210

ODYSSEUS
Done for, old man! Where can we run to?—where?

SILENUS
Into the cave—good hiding-places there.

ODYSSEUS
Not likely!—to walk straight into the snare

SILENUS
Quite likely. Plenty of rat-holes there, my boy.

ODYSSEUS
Never! 'twould stain my laurels won at Troy   215
To run from one man. I stood under shield
Against a host of Trojans in the field.
If I must die, I'll die in a blaze of glory.
Or live, and be yet more renowned in story.   219

                              (Enter CYCLOPS,
                              ODYSSEUS, and his
                              men shrink away to
                              one side. SILENUS
                              slips into cave.)

CYCLOPS
Now then! Come, come, What's this? What, standing round
All idle, revelling! Don't think you have found
Your Bacchus here! No brazen clashing comes
Of cymbals here, nor thump of silly drums.
Here, how about those kids of mine, those lambs?
Are they all sucking, nuzzling at their dams?   225
What have you done with all the milk you drew
For cheese? Are those rush-crates brim-full?—
   speak, you!
Why don't you answer? Where's that stick?—I'll drown
Your eyes with tears! Look up, and don't look down!

CHORUS
          (Pointing their noses at the sky.)
Oh, please! I'm looking at great Zeus this minute: 230
I see Orion's belt, and seven stars in it.

CYCLOPS
And where's my breakfast? What, not ready yet?

CHORUS
Quite ready. Hope your gullet's quite sharp-set.

CYCLOPS
Are the bowls ready yet for me to swig?

CHORUS
Drink, if you like, a hogshead—
                (Aside.)
   like a pig!   235

CYCLOPS
(Looks at bowls.)
Ewes' milk, or cows', or half-and-half, are these?

CHORUS
Whichever you like—but don't swig me up, please?

CYCLOPS
Not I! Fine rumpus would my belly feel—
You capering there, and going toe-and-heel!
                    (Sees ODYSSEUS and his men.)
Hullo! what's this here rabble at my door?   240
Have thieves or pirates run their ship ashore?
And what?—these lambs—they're *my* lambs, taken out
From *my* caves, and with plaited withs about
Their bodies coiled!—what, bowls with cheeses packed?
And here's my old man with his bald pate cracked!   245

              (SILENUS comes out of cave,
               artistically made up as victim of
               assault and battery.)

SILENUS
Oh! oh! They've pummelled me into a fever!

CYCLOPS
Who? Who has punched your head, you old deceiver?

SILENUS
These rogues. I tried to stop their robbing you.

CYCLOPS
What? I'm a God, a God's son! Sure, they knew?

SILENUS
Yes, I kept telling them; but still they hauled   250
The goods out; and they gobbled—though I bawled
"You mustn't!"— gobbled up your cheese, and stole
All these dear little lambs; and, on my soul,
They swore they'd tie a long rope round your waist,
And rip your noble guts out, give you a taste   255
Of whip-lash, flay your royal back, my lord.
Of all the skin, then bind you, drag you aboard
Their ship, and tumble you into the hold.
And take you overseas. Sir, to be sold
There to some quarryman, to heave big stones,   260
Or grind in some corn-mill with weary bones.

CYCLOPS

Oh, did they? Just you look sharp, then, and set
A fine edge on my carving-knives, and get
A good big faggot on the hearth, and start
The fire; and these shall promptly do their part   265
Of filling up my crop. Hot from the embers
I'll eat them. I'm the carver who dismembers
My game, and I'm the cook who does the boiling
And stewing here! My appetite's been spoiling
For something of a change from one long run   270
Of mountain-game: my stomach's overdone
with lion-steaks and venison. Now for a taste
Of man!—I don't know when I ate one last.

SILENUS

Yes, Master; the same dishes every day
Do pall, and change is pleasant, as you say;   275
Yes, and it's quite an age since guests like these
Have sought your cave's fine hospitalities.

ODYSSEUS

Cyclops, do let the strangers make reply.
We wanted food, and so we came to buy
Some at your cave: we came from yonder ship.   280
And this fat rogue was ready, for a sip
Of wine, to sell these lambs: he got one drink
As earnest money, and straightway, in a wink,
He offered us the lot, of his own accord.
We never laid a finger on him, my lord.   285
All that he's said to you was one big lie
To excuse his selling your goods on the sly.

SILENUS

I?—devil take you!

ODYSSEUS

If I'm lying now.

SILENUS

By the Sea-god your father. Sir, I vow.   290
By mighty Triton, Nereus, Lord of Waters,
Calypso, and all Nereus' pretty daughters,
By every holy wave that swings and swishes—
In short, by all the gods and little fishes
I swear—my beautiful! my Cyclops sweet!   295
My lordykin! I never sold one bleat
Of all your flocks! Else—may they go to hell,

These bad boys, whom their father loves so well!

CHORUS

Go there yourself! I saw you with these eyes
Trading with them. And if I'm telling lies,   300
May father burn for ever and a day!
Sir, don't you do the strangers wrong, I pray!

CYCLOPS

You're liars! As for me, I'd sooner credit
What he says, than if Rhadamanthus said it;
I call him the more righteous of the two.   305
But now I'll question this same stranger-crew:—
Where did you sail from, strangers? What's your nation?
In what town did you get your education?

ODYSSEUS

We're Ithacans born and bred: from Ilium—
After destroying the city—we have come   310
To this your land, being driven tempest-tossed
Out of our course, Sir Cyclops, to your coast.

CYCLOPS

Oho I then you're the men who went in search
Of Helen, who left her husband in the lurch.
And ran away to Ilium by Scamander?   315

ODYSSEUS

Yes: slippery fish—hard work to hook and land her.

CYCLOPS

(With air of virtuous indignation.)
Yes—and a most disgraceful exhibition
You made of your own selves!—an expedition
To Phrygia, for one petticoat!—disgusting!

ODYSSEUS

Don't blame us men: it was the Gods' on-thrusting.   320
But, noble son of the great Lord of Sea,
We beg you, we beseech you earnestly,—
Don't be so cruel as to kill and feast,
with cannibal jawbones, like a godless beast.
On guests, whose claims you surely will not spurn!   325
Lord king, we've done your father a good turn:
We've saved his temples for him in every corner
Of all Greece: after this, no pirate scorner
Of holy things will smash his temple-doors

On the Taenarian haven's peaceful shores;
And upon Malea's height his holy fane
Is safe now, and the rocks of silver vein
On Sunium— Athena's property,—
And on Geraestus his great sanctuary.
In fact, we put our foot down—wouldn't stand
The intolerable reproach on Hellas-land
Brought by those Phrygian thieves. And in the fruits
Of this you share; for here by Etna's roots.
Below his rocky lava-welling dome,
Just on the skirts of Greece you have your home.
And 'tis the law of nations
                    (Cyclops yawns.)
—if may
Ask your attention to the words I say—
To welcome suppliant castaways—indeed,
To give them gifts, and fresh rig-outs at need.
Not stick their limbs on great ox-roasting spits
To cram your jaws and belly with tit-bits.
Enough has Priam's land bereaved our Hellas
By drinking blood of thousands slain, as well as
By widowing wives, and robbing grey-haired mothers
And fathers of their sons. Now, if the others.
The few survivors, are to be by you
Roasted for horrible feastings, whereunto
Shall one for justice look? Hear reason and right,
Cyclops; restrain your savage appetite:
Choose fear of God for godlessness! A host
Of men, in making sinful gains, have lost.

SILENUS

Now just take my advice:—of this chap's meat
Don't leave one scrap. And if you also eat
His nice long tongue, you'll grow as smart as he
In making speeches, and in repartee.

CYCLOPS

Wealth, master Shrimp, is to the truly wise
The one true god; the rest are mockeries
Of tall talk, naught but mere word-pageantries.
As for my father's fanes by various seas.
That for them!—why d'ye talk to me of these?
And as for Zeus's thunder—I've no fear
Of that, sir stranger! it's by no means clear
To me that he's a mightier god than I;
So I don't care for him; I'll tell you why:—
When he pours down his rain from yonder sky,

I have snug lodgings in this cave of mine.
On roasted veal or some wild game I dine,
Then drench my belly, sprawling on my back.
with a whole butt of milk. His thunder-crack— 375
I answer it, when he splits the clouds asunder.
with boomings of my cavern-shaking thunder.
And when the north-east wind pours down the snow,
I wrap my body round with furs, and so
I light my fire, and naught for snow I care. 380
And, willy-nilly, earth has got to bear
The grass that makes my sheep and cattle fat.
I sacrifice to my great Self, sir Sprat,
And to no god beside—except, that is.
My belly, greatest of all deities. 385
Eat plenty and drink plenty every day.
And never worry—*that* is, so I say.
The Zeus that suits a level-headed man;
But as for those who framed an artful plan
Of laws, to puzzle plain men's lives with these— 390
I snap ray thumb at them. I'll never cease
Seeking my own soul's good—by eating you.
And, as for guest-gifts, you shall have your due—
Oh no, I won't be niggard!—a hot fire.
And yonder caldron, which my Sea-god sire 395
Will fill up with his special private brew
To make your chop-steaks into a savoury stew
Now, toddle in, and all stand ready near
The Paunch-god's altar, and make your host good cheer.

(Begins to drive the crew in.)

ODYSSEUS

Alas! through Trojan conflicts have I won 400
And perils of the sea, only to run
Aground on a godless villain's evil will.
And on his iron-bound heart my life to spill!
O Pallas, Child of Zeus, O Heavenly Queen,
Help, help me now, for never have I been. 405
Mid all Troy's travail, in such strait as this!
Oh, this is peril's bottomless abyss
O Dweller in the starry Halls of Light,
Zeus, thou Guest-champion, look upon my plight!
If thou regard not, vainly we confess 410
Thy godhead, Zeus, who art mere nothingness!

(Follows his men into the cave,
followed by CYCLOPS.)

CHORUS

Gape wide your jaws, you one-eyed beast.
　　Your tiger-fangs, an' a' that;
Hot from the coals to make your feast
　　Here's roast, an' boiled, an' a' that.
For a' that, an' a' that.
His guid fur-rug, an' a' that.
He's tearin', champin' flesh o' guests!
　　So nane for me, for a' that.

Ay, paddle your ain canoe, One-eye,
　　Wi' bluidy oars, an' a' that;
Your impious hall, I pass it by!
　　I cry "avaunt!" for a' that.
For a' that, an' a' that,
Your "Etna Halls," an' a' that,
You joy in gorgin' strangers' flesh.
　　Awa' wi' ye, for a' that!

A heartless wretch is he, whoe'er.
　　When shipwrecked men, an' a' that.
Draw nigh his hearth wi' suppliant prayer,
　　Slays, eats them up, an' a' that.
For a' that an' a' that,
His stews an' steaks, an' a' that,
His teeth are foul wi' flesh o' man!
　　He's damned to hell, for a' that!

(Enter ODYSSEUS
from cave.)

ODYSSEUS

Oh God, that cave!—that mine eyes should behold
Horrors incredible, things that might be told
In nightmare demon-legends, never found
In acts of men!

CHORUS

What is it? Has that hound
Of hell yet feasted on your friends, poor man?

ODYSSEUS

Yes, two. He glared on all; then he began
To weigh them in his hands, to find out who
Were fattest and best-nourished of my crew!

CHORUS

Poor soul! How did your sufferings befall?   445

ODYSSEUS

When in yon dungeon he had herded all,
He kindled first a fire, and then hurled down
On that broad hearth a tall oak's branching crown,
A mass of wood three waggons scarce could bear;
Then he spread out, hard by the red flame's glare,   450
A deep broad bed of fallen leaves of pine.
Next, with the milk he drew from all his kine
He filled a ninety-gallon cask: beside
This tank he set a bowl some five feet wide,
And, by the looks, 'twas more than two yards deep;   455
Then round his brazen caldron made flames leap.
Next got his spits out, limbs of blackthorn roughly
Trimmed with a bill, the points fire-hardened toughly;
Then, bowls to hold the blood made forth to well
By cleavers of this fiend of Etna's hell.   460
When all was ready for this devil-cook
God-hated, with a sudden snatch he took
Two of my comrades, and, as one might beat
A hideous music out, so did he treat
These in the killing: one man's head he swung   465
Against the caldron's brass that hollow rung;
By the heel-sinew he gripped the other, dashed
The wretch against a sharp rock-spur, and splashed
His brains all round: then with swift savage knife
Sliced off the flesh yet quivering with life: 470
He set some o'er the fire on spits to broil,
And into his caldron flung whole limbs to boil,
Then I—oh misery!—shedding tear on tear
To wait upon this Cyclop fiend drew near;
While all the rest in crannies of the rock   475
with bloodless faces cowered, like a flock
Of scared birds. When he had gorged himself at last
with my friends' flesh, he flung him down; a blast
Of foul breath from his throat burst loathsomely.
Then a great inspiration came to me: 480
with Maron's mighty wine I filled a cup,
And offered it, saying, as I held it up,
"Son of the Sea-king, Cyclops, taste and know
What heavenly draughts from vines of Hellas flow.
This is the glory of our Vineyard-lord."   485
And he, gorged with that banqueting abhorred.
Took it, and swilled it all down at one draught.
Up went his praising hands: "Dear, guest," he laughed,

"With glorious drink you crown a glorious feast!"
So when I saw how much it pleased the beast,   490
I filled his cup again, for well I knew
The wine would trip him up, and full soon too
Would give me my revenge. And now he roared
Forth into singing: still I poured and poured
Cup after cup, till glowed his villain bowels   495
with that good liquor. Dissonant rang his howls
By my men's moans and sobs, and all about
The cavern echoed. I have stolen out,
And mean, if you are willing, to rescue you
And myself too. Say, what d'you mean to do?   500
Do you, or do you not, consent to flee
From this inhospitable brute, and be
Dwellers henceforth in Bacchus' halls afar—
Where also the sweet Fountain-maidens are?
Your father in there—well, he did approve;   505
But he's too weak to help: he's fallen in love,
Moreover, with the wine, can think of naught
But trying to get his share. His wings are caught.
As if with birdlime, by the cup: his wit
Is all abroad. But you are young and fit: 510
Escape with me, and meet your dear old lord
Dionysus—how unlike yon brute abhorred!

                          CHORUS
O dearest friend, that I might flee away
From godless Goggle-eye, and see that day!
The pipe of pleasure has for long been pining.   515
For on no dainty things have I been dining.

                          ODYSSEUS
Hear then, the vengeance that it's in my mind
To wreak upon that scoundrel beast, and find
Therein your own escape from slavery.

                          CHORUS
O speak! Not more delightfully to me   520
The music of an Indian harp would sound
Than tidings of his death—the Cyclop hound!

                          ODYSSEUS
He wants to go forth, full of wine and glee,
To his brother Cyclops for wild revelry.

                          CHORUS
I see—you ambush him in some lone copse.   525

Or,—one sly push, and over the cliff he drops.

ODYSSEUS

No, no; my trick is artfuller by far.

CHORUS

What? Long ago I heard how 'cute you are.

ODYSSEUS

I'll put him off this revel-game; I'll say
He shouldn't give such wine as this away   530
To his fellow-beasts, but keep it, only thinking
Of having a high old time of private drinking.
And, when he's sleeping, Bacchus' captive, then—
A stake of olive lies in yonder den:
My sword shall shape to a point yon bit of tree;   535
I'll thrust it in the fire; and when I see
That it is well ablaze, I'll whip the thing
Out, and all glowing-red I'll slip the thing
Into the middle of Master Cyclops' eye.
And melt his vision out with fire thereby.   540
And, just as shipwrights fitting beams together
Will twirl the big drill with long straps of leather.
So in this fellow's eye I'll twirl about
My firebrand till I scorch his eyeball out.

CHORUS

Callooh! Callay!   545
I'm glad—I'm mad with joy at your invention!

ODYSSEUS

Then in my black ship it is my intention
To put your father you, and my friends freed:
Then with oars double-manned away we speed.

CHORUS

And in the handling of this burning brand   550
That scoops his eye out, can't I bear a hand,
Just as in sacrifices all have part?
I'll take my little share with all my heart.

ODYSSEUS

O yes, you must: the brand is monstrous great,   555
And all must help at it.

CHORUS

                I'd lift a weight

Enough for a hundred carts, if so I might.
As one burns out a wasps' nest, quench the light
Of One-eye—damn him down to lowest hell!   560

ODYSSEUS

Now, mum's the word! You know the trick right well;
So, when I call on you, do you obey
The master-mind—that's me. No running away
For me, to save myself, and leave my crew
Inside! I *might* escape: I got clear through   565
A tunnel in the rock with small ado.
But—give my friends the slip, with whom I came
Here, and escape alone!—'twould be a shame!

(Exit into cave.)

CHORUS

O who, and O who will come and take his stand.
And grip the shaft and plunge beneath his brow the
    glowing brand?   570
And it's O, but a Cyclop with eye on fire is grand!

(Sound of singing in cave.)

O hush and O hush! for he howls a drunken song,
A hideous discord bellowed by an unmelodious tongue.
And it's O, but his music shall turn to wails ere long!
He comes, O he comes; he has left his cave behind.   575
Some revel-song adapted to his thick head let us find.
And it's O, but for certain he'll very soon be blind.

(Enter CYCLOPS with
ODYSSEUS and
SILENUS.)

CHORUS [CON'T]
O bliss to be chanting the Song of the Wine,
    When the cluster's fountain is flowing,
When your soul floats forth on the revel divine.   580
    And your love in your arms is glowing,
When you play with the odorous golden hair
    Of a fairy-like sweet wee love,
And you murmur through shining curls the prayer—
    "Unlock love's door unto me, love!"   585

CYCLOPS
Oho! Oho! I am full of good drink.

   Full of glee from a good feast's revel!
I'm a ship that is laden till ready to sink
   Right up to my crop's deck-level!
The jolly spring season is tempting me out
   To dance on the meadow-clover
with my Cyclop brothers in revel-rout —
   Here, hand the wine-skin over

CHORUS

With eyes lit up with the love-light's spell
   From his halls is the bridegroom pacing,—
"O, somebody loves me, but I won't tell!"—
   And the bridal-torch is blazing.
O the warm warm clasp of a glowing bride
   In the cave, and the fervid bosom!
O the garland of roses and paeonies pied
   That around thy brows shall blossom

ODYSSEUS

Cyclop, heed me, for I know all about
This Wine-god in the cup that you've drained out.

CYCLOPS

Who is this Bacchus?—not a real god, is he?

ODYSSEUS

In giving men good times there's none so busy.

CYCLOPS

I belch him out, and find that very pleasant.

ODYSSEUS

That's him—hurts nobody—it shows he's present.

CYCLOPS

How does this god like lodging in a skin?

ODYSSEUS

He's all serene wherever you stick him in.

CYCLOPS

Gods shouldn't wear hide-jackets: that's my view.

ODYSSEUS

Pho! if you like him, what's his coat to you?

CYCLOPS
Can't say I like the skin: the drink is prime.

ODYSSEUS
Now just stop here, and have a high old time.

CYCLOPS
What?—give my brethren none of this rich hoard?

ODYSSEUS
Keep it for your own drinking, like a lord.   615

CYCLOPS
But it's more neighbourly to share with friends.

ODYSSEUS
Well, revelling in blows and brawling ends.

CYCLOPS
I'm drunk; but none dare touch me! I'm all right.

ODYSSEUS
My dear Sir, home's the place when one is tight.

CYCLOPS
Not revel after a booze?—that's silly, very!   620

ODYSSEUS
Wise men stay indoors when wine makes them merry.

CYCLOPS
Shall I stay in, Silenus? What d'ye think?

SILENUS
Stay. Why have other noses in your drink?

CYCLOPS
Well, to be sure, this long thick grass is fine.

SILENUS
Yes, and it's nice to drink in warm sunshine.   625
Down with you then, in lordly ease to lie.

        (Slides wine-bowl behind CYCLOP'S
        back.)

CYCLOPS
Now then, you've put that bowl behind me!—why?

SILENUS
Lest some one passing by us might upset it.

CYCLOPS
Ha, I know better! You are trying to get it
For stolen drinks. Just set it in full view.   630
Now, stranger, what's to be my name for you?

ODYSSEUS
Nobody. Haven't you a gift for me
To bless you for?

CYCLOPS
                Of all your company
I'll feast on you the last.   635

SILENUS
                O Cyclops, best
Of hosts, a noble gift you give your guest!

(Stealthily drinks.)

CYCLOPS
Ah! what are you up to?—drinking on the sly!

SILENUS
No, no: the wine kissed me, so fair am I.

CYCLOPS
I'll teach you, if you make love to the wine   640
Which loves you not!

SILENUS
                It does: these charms of mine,
It says, have won its heart.

CYCLOPS
                Here, fill the cup.
Pour in—up to the brim. Now, hand it up.   645

SILENUS
Is it the proper mixture?—let me see.

(Stoops his face to bowl.)

CYCLOPS

You'll be the death of me! Quick, hand it me
Just as it is!

SILENUS
(Puts wreath on CYCLOPS' head,
so as to cover his eye.)
By Jove, no! I must first
Crown with this wreath your brow, and—quench my
    thirst,

(Drinks.)

CYCLOPS

You thieving cupbearer!

SILENUS

Good heavens! not so.
You *should* say, "You delicious wine!" you know.
Now let me wipe your nose, that you may sip
Your wine genteelly.

CYCLOPS
    Go along! my lip
And my moustache are clean enough for me.

SILENUS

Now sink down on your elbow gracefully;
        (Cyclops rolls on his back.)
Then drain the cup, just as you see me do—
I mean, just as you don't.

(Takes a big drink.)

CYCLOPS
(Sitting up.)
    Hi! stop there, you!
What are you up to?

SILENUS

A bumper! Joys untold.

CYCLOPS

Here, stranger, be my cupbearer. Catch hold!

ODYSSEUS

The wine knows me: my hand brings out its savour.

CYCLOPS

Fill up.

ODYSSEUS

All right. Don't talk—you'll miss the flavour.

CYCLOPS

Can't help but talk, with a pailful in one's crop.

ODYSSEUS

Here, tip it off. Mind, don't you leave one drop.
The rule is, don't give in until the wine
Gives out.

CYCLOPS
(Drinks.)
Oh my! a clever tree that vine
Must be!

ODYSSEUS
And if you pour full bumpers down
On top of a full meal and fairly drown
The thirst out of your paunch, 'twill veil your eye
with sweet sleep. If the cup be not drained dry,
Bacchus will parch your throat most damnably,

CYCLOPS
(Buries his face in bowl.)
Oho! oho! I've dived deep into this,
And just come up again! Unmingled bliss!
I see heaven floating down, blended in one
with earth below! I see Zeus on his throne,
And all the Gods, the holy heavenly faces!
No, I won't kiss you!—that's the naughty Graces
Tempting me. Ganymede will do for me!
(Seizes SILENUS.)
I've got him here; and, by the Graces Three,
I'll have a lovely time with him; I care
Never a straw for all the female fair.

SILENUS

What? what? Are you Zeus, and I Ganymede?

CYCLOPS
(Catching him up.)
Yes!—up from Troy I snatch you—yes indeed!

SILENUS

Boys! murder! help! I'm in an awful plight!

CHORUS

What?—scorn your lover?—snub him 'cause he's tight?

SILENUS

This wine is bitter beer!—O cursed spite!

(CYCLOPS staggers
into cave, with
SILENUS under his
arm.)

ODYSSEUS

Come, Bacchus children, brave lads, up, be doing!
Our foe's in there! Right soon will he be spewing   695
Gobbets of flesh from a shameless gullet deep,
Sprawling upon his back in drunken sleep.
The stake in there jets forth a fiery fume.
All's ready for the last act, to consume
The Cyclops' eye with fire. Be men!   700

CHORUS

We pant
To show a soul of rock, of adamant!
In then, before our father come to grief.
We're ready all to follow you, our chief,

ODYSSEUS

O Fire-god, king of Etna, burn away   705
The eye of thy vile neighbour, and for aye
Rid thee of him! O child of black Night, Sleep,
On this god-hated brute in full power leap!
Bring not Odysseus and his crew to naught,
After those glorious toils in Ilium wrought.   710
Through one who gives to God nor man a thought!
Else must we think that Chance bears rule in heaven,
That lordship over Gods to her is given.

(Exit into cave.)

CHORUS

As I cam' through a cave's gate,
A slaves' gate, a knave's gate,   715
A "Shipwrecked Sailors' Grave's" gate,
    I heard a caldron sing—

"O weel may the fire glow, the reek blow, the stake go!
O weel may his throat crow for the eye that flames are in!"
  And it's O for my Lord's shout ringing,   720
   For the singing, the swinging
   Dance, for the ivy clinging!
    And good-bye to the desolate shore!
So weel may the wine flow, and lay low our brute foe,
To wake up in mad throe, in darkness evermore!   725

                   (Re-enter ODYSSEUS
                   from cave.)

ODYSSEUS

Hush, you wild things, for Heaven's sake!—still as death!
Shut your lips tight together!—not a breath!
Don't wink, don't cough, for fear the beast should wake
Ere we twist out his eye with that red stake.

CHORUS

We are mum: we clench our teeth tight on the air.   730

ODYSSEUS

Now then, in with you! Grasp the brand in there
with brave hands: glowing red-hot is the tip.

CHORUS
(Edging away.)
You, please, appoint who must be first to grip
The burning stake, and scorch out Cyclops' eye.
That all may share the grand chance equally.   735

A SATYR

Oh, we—too far outside the door we are!—
Can't reach his eye—can't poke the fire so far.

ANOTHER SATYR

And we—O dear, we've fallen lame just now!

ANOTHER SATYR

And so have we: we've sprained—I can't tell how—
Our ankles, standing here. Oh my poor foot!   740

ODYSSEUS

Sprained standing still?

ANOTHER SATYR

Oh dear! a lot of soot,

Or dust, into our eyes the wind has brought!

ODYSSEUS

The cowards! At a pinch they're good for naught

CHORUS

Because I have compassion on my back,   745
And don't want all my teeth by one big smack
Knocked down my throat, d'ye call that cowardice?
Look here—I know a song of Orpheus's,
A lovely incantation! 'twill constrain
The stake to plunge itself into his brain.   750
And burn the giant's eye out—a grand song!

ODYSSEUS

Poor chicken-hearts! I knew you all along.
I'll do what's better; use my trusty crew—
Indeed I've no choice. There's no fight in you:
Still, cheer us on with some good rousing chanty.   755
And screw to the sticking-point our courage, can't ye?

(Enters cave.)

CHORUS

Instead of the tongs, sir, dear pussy's paw, sir, will
   get my chestnuts out very well;
But, as far as a song, sir, can go, old Saucer-eye shall
   frizzle in flames of hell.
      So yeo-heave-ho! and in she'll go!
Give way, my hearties! Put your backs to it! Stick
   to the work!—   760
A brave tar's part is to stick like wax to it—never
   a shirk!
      Burn out his eye, sir, the gormandizer.
      Who goes and fries, sir, the trustful stranger!
      with a red-hot poker make him a smoker
      Like Etna—the soaker, the sheepwalk-ranger!   765

         (ODYSSEUS and his men bring the
          burning stake, and plunge it into
          the CYCLOPS' eye.)

      In you go quick with it!—twirl it about!
      You've done the trick with it I—now whip it out
      Ere he catch you a lick with it a terrible clout;
      For he feels pretty sick with it—of that there's
         no doubt.

CYCLOPS
(Starting up.)
Ah-h! my eye's turned to a red-hot coal! Oh my!   770

CHORUS
Well sung! Encore! Encore, old Saucer-eye!

CYCLOPS
Oh! blackguard villains! Oh! They've done for me
Don't think to escape, you paltry rascalry.
Out of this cave, and laugh at me! I'll stand
Here, barring the only door with either hand,   775

CHORUS
Why bawl so, Goggle-eye?

CYCLOPS
I'm kilt intirely!

CHORUS
You do look bad,

CYCLOPS
What's more, I feel so—direly!

CHORUS
You fell face down in the fire when you were tight?   780

CYCLOPS
No!—Nobody's killed me!

CHORUS
No?—then you're all right.

CYCLOPS
Nobody's blinded me!

CHORUS
Then you can't be blind.

CYCLOPS
I wish you were!   785

CHORUS
Please make it to my mind
Quite clear, how nobody could poke your eye out.

CYCLOPS
You're chaffing me! Where's Nobody?

CHORUS
          Don't cry out.
Because he's nowhere, Blunderbore—don't you see?

CYCLOPS
I tell you again, that stranger's murdered me.
The dirty spalpeen, who drenched me with drink!

CHORUS
Ah, wine's the chap to trip your legs, I think.

CYCLOPS
For Heaven's sake tell me—are they still inside?
Or have they got away?

CHORUS
          They're trying to hide
Under that rock-ledge: they stand silent there.

CYCLOPS
On which side of me?

CHORUS
          On your right.

CYCLOPS
          Oh where?

CHORUS
Close up against the rock. Ha!—got the lot?

                    (CYCLOPS makes a mild plunge, and
                    dashes his head, against the rock.
                    Some of the crew slip out.)

CYCLOPS
Oh misery on misery! I've caught
My head a bang that's split it!

CHORUS
          What?—slipped clear
Between your fingers?

CYCLOPS
(Groping with his hands.)
I can't find them here!
You said they *were* here?

CHORUS

No, *this* side I told you.

CYCLOPS

Where? where?

CHORUS
Whisk round!—to your left! Aha!   810
they've sold you!

(The last of the crew slip by.)

CYCLOPS
You're laughing at me!—jeering at my woes!

CHORUS
No, no! Look! Nobody's right before your nose!

CYCLOPS
(Making plunge at nothing.)
Villain! where are you?

ODYSSEUS
Out of reach, I assure ye,   815
I ward Odysseus' body from your fury.

CYCLOPS
What?—a new name?—that doesn't sound the same!

ODYSSEUS
My father called me Odysseus: that's my name.
And so you thought that you'ld get off scot-free
For your unhallowed feast! A shame 'twould be   820
If, after burning Troy I took on you
No vengeance for the murder of my crew!

CYCLOPS
Woe's me! the ancient prophecy comes true
Which said that you would blind me on your way
Homeward from Troy. Ha! this too did it say,   825
That you'ld be punished for this wrong to me,
Tossed through long years about the homeless sea.

ODYSSEUS

I laugh to scorn your bodings. I have done
All that your prophet said. Now will I run
My good ship's keel adown the sloping strand;   830
Then, ho for Sicily's sea and fatherland!

CYCLOPS

Not you! I'll tear this rock up, hurl, and smash
You and your men all to a bloody mash!
I'll climb a crag, and do it. Though I'm blind,
My way out through this rifted rock I'll find.   835

CHORUS

We will sail with Odysseus from this shore,
And serve Lord Bacchus henceforth evermore.   837

(Exeunt omnes,
leaving CYCLOPS
groping and
stumbling amongst
the rocks.)

(LIGHTS FADE.)

(CURTAINS.)

(END OF PLAY.)

CYCLOPS

Translated by

Theodore Alois Buckley

PERSONS REPRESENTED

SILENUS

CHORUS OF SATYRS

ULYSSES

CYCLOPS

THE ARGUMENT

On the return of Ulysses from Troy, he was driven to Sicily, where Polyphemus and the Cyclops dwelt. Meeting with Silenus and the Satyrs, who had been enslaved to Polyphemus, he sought to purchase meat and cheese in exchange for wine. Polyphemus entering, Silenus accused Ulysses of stealing, and offering violence to himself and companions. All would have perished, but that Ulysses and his sailors bored out the one eye of the sleeping Polyphemus, and thereby escaped, liberating the Satyrs. The plot is entirely Homeric.

SILENUS

O Bromius, through thee I have ten thousand toils, both now, and when my body was hale in youth. First indeed, when, maddened by Juno, thou wentest away, deserting thy nurses, the mountain nymphs; and afterwards being an assistant to thee on thy right hand in the conflict of the spear with the earth-born race, having smitten Enceladus on the midst of his shield, I slew him with my spear. Come, let me see, do I speak of this, having seen a dream? No, by Jove, since indeed I showed even the spoils to Bacchus. And now I am exhausting a labor greater than those. For after Juno had excited against thee a Tyrrhenian race of pirates, that thou mightest be sold far off, I, having learned the news, sail with my children in quest of thee. But myself taking the two-handled tiller at the extremity of the stern, steered, and my children sitting at the oars, whitening with oars the deep-blue sea, sought thee, O king. But just as we had sailed near to Malea, an Eastern blast, blowing down upon our ship, drove us upon this rock of Aetna, where the one-eyed sons of the ocean God, the Cyclops, dwell in desert caves, slayers of men.   18

Being taken captives by one of these we are slaves in his house; and they call him, whom we serve, Polyphemus. But instead of Bacchanalian revels we feed the flocks of the impious Cyclops. My children indeed, youths born, are tending sheep on the distant downs; but I remaining (at home) am appointed to fill the troughs, and sweep this house, as the servant to the unholy Cyclops at his impious feasts. And now the enjoined command must needs be (done), that I sweep the dwelling with this iron rake, (and) that we may receive my absent master, the Cyclops, and his sheep, in clean caves. But already I perceive my sons draw nigh, tending upon their flocks. What is this? Is this your noise now like that of the Sicinnides, when, accompanying me in Bacchic revelry to the house of Althtaea, ye drew nigh, wantoning in strains of the lyre?   32

CHORUS

Whither indeed for me dost thou, born of noble sires, and sprung from noble parents, whither indeed for me dost thou bound o'er the rocks? Here is no gentle gale, or grassy herbage; but the eddying water of the rivers lies in the troughs near the caves, where are the bleatings of thy young.

Ho! ho! not here, not here shalt thou feed? Wilt thou not rather to the dewy slope? Ho! I will soon cast a stone at thee, get thee gone, O get thee gone, thou horned one, to the stall of the sheep-pasturing wild Cyclops. Relax for me your swollen udders, receive to your breasts your offspring whom

ye leave in the beds of the lambs. The bleatings of your little young ones day-slumbering yearn for you. 43
   Will you ever return within the Aetnean rocks, having quitted the grassy pastures? These things are not Bacchus, these are not dances and thyrsus-bearing Bacchants, not the clang of cymbals by stream-pouring fountains, not the fresh drippings of wine, or Nesa with the nymphs. To Venus I sing a hymn, Iacchus, Iacchus! (Venus,) whom chasing I flew with the white-footed Bacchants. O friend, O thou dear Bacchus, whither dost thou saunter alone, waving thy auburn locks? But I, thy attendant, am a slave to a one-eyed Cyclops, wandering a slave in this wretched goat's-skin vest, reft of thy friendship. 53

SILENUS
   Keep silence, O children, and bid your followers collect the flocks into the eaves with rocky roofs.

CHORUS
   Go. But why hast thou this haste, father? 55

SILENUS
   I see on the shore the hull of a Grecian ship, and the rulers of the oars with some chieftain drawing nigh to this cave; and on their necks they carry empty vessels, being in lack of food, and water pitchers, O unhappy strangers! Who can they be? They know not our master Polyphemus, what manner of man he is, having approached this inhospitable roof, and unhappily arrived near this Cyclops' man-devouring jaw. But be quiet, that we may learn whence they are come to the Sicilian rock of Aetna. 63

ULYSSEUS
(Entering.)
   Can ye, strangers, tell whence we may obtain a river draught, a remedy for thirst? Or is any one willing to sell food to mariners in need? What is this? We seem to have entered the city of Bacchus; I behold this troop of Satyrs near the cave. I bid the oldest first "all hail!" 67

SILENUS
   Hail! stranger; but say who thou art, and what is thy country.

ULYSSES
   I am Ulysses of Ithaca, king of the land of the Cephallenians. 70

SILENUS
I know the babbling fellow, the sharp son of Sisyphus.

ULYSSES
That very man am I. Don't be abusive.

SILENUS
From whence sailing comest thou to this Sicilian land?

ULYSSES
From Troy, and the labors at Troy.

SILENUS
How? Didst thou not know the passage to your own fatherland?   75

ULYSSES
A storm of winds drove me hither by violence.

SILENUS
By the Gods! you're exhausting the same fortune as I.

ULYSSES
What, was you, too, brought hither by force?

SILENUS
Pursuing the pirates who carried off Bacchus.

ULYSSES
And what country is this, and who inhabit it?   80

SILENUS
The Aetnean hill, the highest spot in Sicily.

ULYSSES
And where are the walls and fortifications of the city?

SILENUS
There are none; the heights are destitute of men, O
stranger.

ULYSSES
And who possess the land? Is it a race of wild beasts?

SILENUS
The Cyclops dwelling in caves, not in roofed houses.   85

ULYSSES
Obeying whom? Or is the power with the people?

SILENUS
Wandering shepherds; and no one obeys any body in any
thing.

ULYSSES
But do they sow the wheat of Ceres? or on what do they
live?

SILENUS
On milk, and cheeses, and the flesh of sheep.   89

ULYSSES
And have they the cup of Bacchus, the juice of the vine?

SILENUS
By no means. Therefore they inhabit a graceless earth.

ULYSSES
But are they guest-loving and pious in respect to
strangers?

SILENUS
They say that strangers furnish the sweetest meat.

ULYSSES
What sayest thou? Do they rejoice in the flesh of
slaughtered men?

SILENUS
No one has come hither who has not been slaughtered.   95

ULYSSES
But where is the Cyclops himself? Is he within the house?

SILENUS
He is gone towards Aetna, hunting wild beasts with hounds.

ULYSSES
Knowest thou then what thou mayest do, that we may escape
from the land?

SILENUS
I know not, Ulysses; but I would do any thing for you.

ULYSSES
Sell us food, of which we are in need.   100

SILENUS
There is no other, as I said, except flesh.

ULYSSES
But even this is a sweet preventive of hunger.

SILENUS
And there is coagulated cheese, and cows' milk.

ULYSSES
Bear it out; for the light (of day) is fitting for dealings.

SILENUS
But tell me, how much gold wilt thou give instead?   105

ULYSSES
I carry not gold, but the cup of Bacchus.

SILENUS
O thou that tellest of the dearest things, which we long
since lack.

ULYSSES
And truly Maro, the son of the God, gave me the drink.

SILENUS
He whom I once nursed in these arms?   109

ULYSSES
The son of Bacchus, that thou mayest learn more clearly.

SILENUS
Is it aboard the ship, or dost thou bring it?

ULYSSES
This wine-skin, which conceals it as you see, old man.

SILENUS
This would not fill even my mouth.   113

ULYSSES
Ah! but (I have) even twice as much as flows from this
skin.

                         SILENUS
A lovely fountain thou tellest of, and pleasant to me.

                         ULYSSES
Wilt thou that I first give thee a taste of wine unmix'd?

                         SILENUS
It is just; for taste will induce the purchase.   117

                         ULYSSES
And truly I bring a cup together with the skin.

                         SILENUS
Come, pour forth, that I may recollect as I drink.

                         ULYSSES
See!   120

                         SILENUS
O Gods! how sweet an odor it has!

                         ULYSSES
What, didst thou see it?

                         SILENUS
No, by Jove, but I smell it.

                         ULYSSES
Taste then, that thou mayest not praise it from report
alone.

                         SILENUS
O Gods! Bacchus invites me to dance. Hah! hah! Hah!   125

                         ULYSSES
Did it trickle through thy throat nicely for thee.

                         SILENUS
Ay, so that it came to the very tips of my nails.

                         ULYSSES
Besides this we will also give coin.

                         SILENUS
Only open the wine-skin; let the money alone.   129

ULYSSES
Bring out then some cheeses, or the offspring of sheep.

SILENUS
I will do this, caring little for my masters. For I would
readily drain a single cup, giving the cattle of all the
Cyclops in exchange, and cast myself off the White Rock' into
the sea, having once got drunk, and bringing down mine
eyelids. For he, who rejoices not when drinking, is mad, where
it is for this to stand erect, and a handling of breasts, and
a garden is prepared for hands to touch, and dancing too, and
forgetfulness of ill. Shall I then not adore such a cup as
this, bidding the ignorant Cyclops and the eye mid-head weep
to his cost?   139

CHORUS
Listen, Ulysses; let us hold some converse with thee.

ULYSSES
And truly as friends ye confer with a friend.

CHORUS
Did ye take Troy and Helen into your hands?

ULYSSES
Ay, and we have sacked the whole house of the sons of
Priam.   143

SILENUS
Did ye not then, when ye took the young lady, embrace her
all in turn; since indeed she is fond of being married to
many? The traitoress! who, when she saw a person wearing
embroidered drawers around his legs, and a golden collar
around his neck, was all in a flutter, leaving her good little
man Menelaus. Never should this same race of women have been
born — save for me only. See, here is for you food of sheep,
O king Ulysses, a banquet of bleating lambs, and no scarcity
of cheeses of pressed milk. Bear them away; go as quickly as
possible from the cave, having given me in return the juice
of Bacchic clusters.   153

ULYSSES
Alas! hither comes the Cyclops; what shall we do?
For we are undone, O old man; whither must we fly?   155

SILENUS
Within this rock, where indeed ye may lie hid.

ULYSSES
This is terrible that thou sayest, to go within the toils.

SILENUS
It is not terrible. There are many retreats in the rock.

ULYSSES
Not so indeed. For greatly indeed would even Troy moan, if we fly from one man; for I have often with my shield withstood an innumerable crowd of Phrygians. But if we must die, we will die nobly; or living, will well preserve our former renown.   161

CYCLOPS
Hold! give way! what is this? What is this idle riot? Why are ye raving in Bacchic guise? Here is not Bacchus, nor cymbals of brass, nor beatings of drums. How are my young lambkins in the cave? Are they at the breast, or running under the sides of their dams; and is there plenty of cheese pressed out in the wicker vats? What do you say? What speak you? Soon shall some one of you shed tears with (a blow of) this stick. Look up, not down.   168

CHORUS
See! I we are looking up to Jove himself, and I behold the stars and Orion.

CYCLOPS
Is my dinner well got ready?

CHORUS
It is ready. Only let your jaws be ready.

CYCLOPS
Are the bowls also full of milk?

CHORUS
Ay, so that you may suck up a whole tubful, if you wish.

CYCLOPS
Of sheep's milk, or cow's, or both mixed?

CHORUS
Of whatever you please. Only don't swallow me.   175

CYCLOPS

By no means; for dancing in the middle of my paunch, ye
would destroy me by cutting your figures. Ah! what crowd is
this that I see by the stalls? Some pirates or thieves have
landed in the country. I at all events see these lambs from
my caves bound as to their bodies with bent osiers, and the
cheese-vats scattered about, and this old man with his bald
head swollen with blows.   181

SILENUS

Alas! I wretched am being beaten into a fever.

CYCLOPS

By whom? Who has been pummeling thy head, old man?

SILENUS

These men, O Cyclops; because I would not allow them to
plunder your property.   184

CYCLOPS

Knew they not that I was a God, and sprung from Gods?

SILENUS

I told them so; but they carried off your goods, and cat
the cheese, when I did not allow it, and dragged away the
lambs. And they said that, after they had bound you with a
collar three cubits long, they would by force drill out your
entrails through your central eye, and tan your back well for
you with a scourge; and then, having bound you, they would
east you into the deck of their ship, and sell you to
somebody, to heave up stones, or put you to the mill.   192

CYCLOPS

Indeed! Will you not with all haste go and sharpen the
knives, and collecting a mighty pile of fagots, set it on
fire? that being slaughtered forthwith, they may fill my belly
as I eat flesh warm from off the coals for the carver, and
some boiled and sodden in a cauldron; for I am sick of the
mountain-haunting deer; I have banqueted enough on lions and
stags, and it is a long time since I tasted any human flesh.

SILENUS

And truly new things after customary are more pleasant, O
master. For certainly other strangers have not lately come to
these caves.   201

ULYSSES

O Cyclops, hear too the strangers in their turn.

We, desiring to meet with the purchase of food, came nigh thy caves from our ship. But this man sold and gave us lambs in return for a vessel of wine, having received it to drink, willing to us willing; and none of these things was done by violence. But this man says nothing true in what he says, since he was caught selling your goods without your knowledge.

SILENUS

I? A murrain on thee! 208

ULYSSES

If I speak falsely—

SILENUS

By Neptune, who begat thee, O Cyclops, by the great Triton and Nereus, by Calypso and the daughters of Nereus, by the sacred waves and all the race of fishes, I swear, O dearest one, O little Cyclops, O dear little master, that I never sold thy goods to the strangers. Or evilly may perish these evil children mine, whom I most love. 214

CHORUS

Keep thyself quiet! I myself saw thee selling the goods to the strangers. And if I speak falsely, may my lather perish, but do not wrong these strangers.

CYCLOPS

Ye lie. I believe this man more than Rhadamanthus, and say that he is more just. But I wish to ask some questions. From whence have you sailed, O strangers? Of what country are ye? What city has trained you up? 219

ULYSSES

We are of Ithaca by race; and departing from Troy, having sacked the city, we have been cast out, O Cyclops, by the waves of the sea, and are come to thy hind.

CYCLOPS

What, are ye they who went to the city of Troy, neighboring on the Scamander, in a pursuit after the rape of worthless Helen? 223

ULYSSES

The same, having toiled through the terrible trouble.

CYCLOPS

A base expedition, forsooth; ye who for one woman's sake
sailed away to the land of the Phrygians.   225

ULYSSES

It was the will of the deity; charge none of mortals with
it. But we implore thee, O noble son of the marine God—and we
speak like free-men—do not thou endure to slay friends who
have come to thy caves, and place an impious food in thy jaws;
we who have enshrined thy sire, O king, to have the station
of his temple in the recesses of the Grecian land. And the
haven of Taenarus, an unviolated temple, awaits him; and the
extreme recesses of Malea, and the rock of Sunium, with its
silver under it, preserved for Jove-born Minerva, and the
retreats of Geraestus; but we pardoned not to the Phrygians
the foul reproach of Greece. In which matters thou also
sharest, for thou dwellest in Grecian recesses beneath Aetna,
the tire-streaming rock. But turn thou away to the
consideration of human laws, (so as) to receive
shipwreckedsuppliant mariners, and to bestow gifts, and
furnish raiment, and not that they, fixed upon bull-piercing
spits, may fill thy belly and jowls. For enough has the land
of Priam emptied Greece, drinking the blood of many dead,
slain by the spear, and has destroyed widowed wives, and
childless grandams, and hoary sires. But if thou, having burnt
these relics, devour a bitter banquet, whither shall any one
turn? But be persuaded by me, O Cyclops; relax the gluttony
of thy jaw, and prefer piety to impiety; for to many has base
gain brought punishment in exchange.   248

SILENUS

I wish to give this advice. Leave not a morsel of this
fellow's flesh; but if thou eatest his tongue, thou wilt
become a most clever talker, O Cyclops.   250

CYCLOPS

Wealth, my little man, is the deity of the wise; the rest
is a mere brag and fine words. And I bid farewell to the sea-
shore promontories, on which my father is enshrined.   252
Why hast thou set these forward in thy speech? Nor do I
dread the thunderbolt of Jove, O stranger; nor do I know that
Jove is a more potent deity than myself, nor will I care (for
him) in future; and why I care not, hear. When he pours down
rain from above, I have a secure shelter in this rock,
feasting on either a roasted calf, or some savage beast, and
well moistening my supine belly, drinking up a pitcher of
milk, I smite the plain, making a noise in contest with the

thunders ofJove. But when Thracian Boreas pours forth snow, clothing my body in skins of wild beasts, and kindling a fire, I care not for the snow. And the earth of necessity, whether she will or not, bringing forth grass, fattens my flocks, which I sacrifice to no one but myself, and not to the Gods, and to this my belly, the greatest of Gods; for to drink and eat each day, and to give oneself no trouble, this is (the God) Jove for wise men. But they who enacted laws, checkering the life of men, I bid to weep; but I will not cease from indulging my spirit, and eating up thee. And thou shalt receive this hospitable gift, that I may be free from blame; the fire, and this mine ancestral cauldron, which bubbling shall pleasantly receive thy tough flesh. But go ye within, that, standing round the altar (prepared) for the deity within the cave, ye may feast me.   274

ULYSSES

Alas! From the labors of Troy, indeed, and of the sea I have escaped, but now I have met with the disposition and unhospitable heart of an impious man. O Pallas, O mistress, daughter of Jove, now, now give me your aid; for I have come to greater toils and depths of danger than at Troy. And thou, who dwellest in the habitation of the shining stars, O Jove, the guardian of strangers, behold these things; for if thou regardest them not, thou, O Jove, being naught, art vainly esteemed a God.   282

CHORUS

Open the lips of thy wide jaw, O Cyclops, since there is ready for thee (meat) boiled, and roast, and from the coals, to devour, to grind, to mince the limbs of the strangers, cut up on dishes of shaggy hide. Do not, do not, I pray you, betray (me) alone; for (me) alone bring a ship's hull. Adieu to this dwelling, and to the sacrifice which the godless Cyclops of Aetna possesses, rejoicing in the food of strangers' flesh. Cruel the daring wretch, who sacrifices the suppliant hearth-guests of his home, cutting, mincing, and feasting with accursed teeth on the flesh of men warm from the coals.   292

ULYSSES

O Jove, what shall I say? seeing dreadful things within the cave, and not to be believed, like the tales, not the deeds of mortals.

CHORUS

What is it, Ulysses? has the most impious Cyclops been
banqueting on thy dear companions?   295

ULYSSES

Ay, having looked at two of them, and weighed them in his
hands, which had the best-fed thickness of flesh.

CHORUS

How, wretched one, did ye suffer these things?   297

ULYSSES

After we entered into this rocky cave, he first kindled a
fire, casting fagots of the lofty oak upon the wide hearth,
sufficient weight for three wagons to carry. He then spread
his bed of beech leaves on the ground near the flame of the
fire; and filled a cup holding about ten gallons, pouring in
the white milk, after having milked the heifers. And he set
a cup formed of the ivy-tree, of the width of three cubits,
but the depth appeared to be of four. Then he made the brazen
caldron bubble with fire, and (he got ready) spits with the
points burnt with tire, and the other parts polished with the
bill, (formed) of boughs of the christ-thorn, and Aetnean
vessels to receive the blood shed by the jaw of the axe. But
when all things were ready for the God-detested cook of Hades,
having seized on two men of my companions, he slaughtered
them in a certain order, one against the brazen-wrought hollow
of the cauldrons, but seizing the other by the farthest tendon
of his foot, striking indeed against the sharp nail-like point
of a rocky stone, he caused to flow the brain; and having
seized upon the flesh with a savage knife, he roasted it in
the fire; and put some of the limbs into the cauldron to boil.
But I wretched, pouring forth tears from mine eyes,
approached, and ministered to the Cyclops. But the rest, like
birds, kept crouched down in the recesses of the rock, and no
blood was in their skin. But when, sated with the food of my
companions, he fell down, sending forth heavy breathings from
his jaws, some divine counsel inspired me. Having filled
Maro's cup with pure wine, I bring it to him to drink,
speaking thus, "O Cyclops, son of the ocean God, look at this,
how divine a draught Greece obtains from the vine, the juice
of Bacchus." But he, being filled with his shameless repast,
received it, and emptied it, drawing it in without fetching
his breath. And lifting up his hand, he commended (me): "O
dearest of strangers, a glorious cup for a glorious banquet
dost thou give me." But when I perceived that he was
delighted, I gave him another cup, knowing that the wine would

do for him, and that he would soon pay the penalty. And then he betook himself to singing. But I, pouring out one cup after another, warmed his heart with drink. And he sang all out of tune close to my weeping fellow-sailors, and the cave echoed.

But I, stealing out in silence, wish to preserve thee and me, if thou art willing. Say then, whether ye wish or do not wish to escape from this unsocial man, and to dwell in the home of Bacchus along with the Naiad Nymphs? For thy father within approves of this; but he is weak, and caring for naught, through drink, he wavers, having his wing caught by the cup, as if by birdlime. But do you (for you are a sturdy youth) be saved along with me, and recover your old friend Bacchus, not like to the Cyclops. 344

CHORUS

O dearest one, could we but see this day, escaping from the accursed person of the Cyclops; since for a long time we are widowed as to our beloved wine, not being able to escape from this man. 346

ULYSSES

Hear then the revenge I plan against this wicked beast, and the escape from thy slavery.

CHORUS

Speak, for I should not hear more pleasantly the twang of the Asiatic lyre than that the Cyclops was undone.

ULYSSES

Delighted with this draught of Bacchus, he wishes to go to a revel with his brothers.

CHORUS

I understand. You think to slay or cast him down from a precipice, having seized on him alone with ropes. 351

ULYSSES

Nothing of this kind; my device is a crafty one.

CHORUS

How indeed? We have long since heard that thou art clever.

ULYSSES

I will keep him from this revel, saying, that it is not well to give this wine to the Cyclops, but to keep it to himself, and to pass his life pleasantly. But when, overpowered by Bacchus, he sleeps, there is a certain bough of olive in the house, which having sharpened at the tip with this sword, I will put into the fire. And when I see it red hot, taking it up, and driving it hot into the central orb of the Cyclops, I will burn out his eye with the fire. And as a man, in fitting together a ship, drives round and round by the handle the auger with its doubled thongs, so will I whirl round the brand in the light-bearing eye of the Cyclops, and dry up his pupil. 364

CHORUS

Ho! ho! I rejoice, I am mad with thy contrivances.

ULYSSES

And then having embarked thee, and thy friends, and the old man in the hollow hull of the dark ship, I will with a double tier of oars convey you from this land. 367

CHORUS

Can I then, as if after a libation to a God, take hold also of the brand that blinds his eye? For I wish to take part in this slaughter.

ULYSSES

You must do so; for the brand of which we have to take hold together, is great. 370

CHORUS

I would raise it, were it a hundred wagon-loads in weight, if I could tear out, like a swarm of wasps, the eye of the Cyclops about to perish.

ULYSSES

Be silent then, for thou knowest well my stratagem; and when I bid, obey the prime mover of the scheme. For I will not alone be saved, having left my dear friends who are within. And yet I might fly, since I have passed out of the cave's recess; but it is not just to be saved alone, deserting my friends with whom I came hither. 377

SEMICHORUS

Come! Who first? And who appointed after the first, having laid fast hold of the handle of the brand, and driven it within the eyelids of the Cyclops, shall tear out his brilliant eye? 380

SEMICHORUS

Peace! peace! and now drunk, singing an unpleasant tune, the unskilled songster is about to weep, coming out of the rocky dwelling. Come, let us with revels teach the untaught (savage). By all means shall he soon be blind.   383

CHORUS

Blest is he who revels like a Bacchanal, extended out for a revel through the pleasant streams of the grape, fondling in his arms a beloved youth, and on a couch, perfumed with ointment, handling the anointed auburn tresses of a delicate mistress, while he cries out, "Who will open the door for me?"   388

CYCLOPS

Hah! hah! Hal! I full indeed (am I) with wine, and am pleased with the joy of the banquet. Freighted, like a bark of burden, up to the top deck of my belly. But the pleasant grass invites me to the revel in the spring time, to my brother Cyclops. Bear me, O stranger, bear, and give me the wine-skin.   393

CHORUS

Looking pleasantly from his eyes, pleasantly he passes from the house. Some one loves us. But a hostile brand awaits thy person, and like a tender nymph is within the dewy cave. And not one tint of crowns shall shortly surround thy head.

ULYSSES

Cyclops, listen; for 1 am experienced in the wine which I gave thee to drink.   397

CYCLOPS

And what God is Bacchus held to be?

ULYSSES

The greatest to men for delight of life.

CYCLOPS

I therefore throw him up pleasantly.   400

ULYSSES

Such is the God; he hurts none of mortals.

CYCLOPS

But how can a God rejoice at having his abode in a skin?

                    ULYSSES
Wherever any one places him, there he is well suited.

                    CYCLOPS
It behooves not the Gods to have a habitation in skins.

                    ULYSSES
But what matter, if it delight thee? Is the skin
disagreeable to thee?   405

                    CYCLOPS
I hate the skin, but I love this cup.

                    ULYSSES
Remain then and drink, and please yourself, O Cyclops.

                    CYCLOPS
Must I not share this drink with my brothers?

                    ULYSSES
(No,) for by keeping it yourself, you will appear more
honorable.

                    CYCLOPS
But more useful, by giving it to my friends.   410

                    ULYSSES
A revel loves fisticuffs, and abusive strife.

                    CYCLOPS
Granted I am drunk. But no one on earth would touch me.

                    ULYSSES
My good friend, it behooves one who has been drinking, to
remain at home.

                    CYCLOPS
A dolt is he, who having drunk, loves not reveling.

                    ULYSSES
But whoever being drunk remains at home, is wise.   415

                    CYCLOPS
What shall we do, O Silenus? Do you think we should remain?

ULYSSES

I think so; for what need is there of fellow-wassailers, O
Cyclops.

CYCLOPS

And truly the ground of the flowery grass is covered with
down.

SILENUS

Ay, and 'tis delightful to drink in the warmth of the sun.
Sit down then by me, resting thy side on the ground.

CYCLOPS

See! why indeed dost thou set the cup behind me?   420

SILENUS

That no one should come and lay hold of it.

CYCLOPS

No, it is that you want to drink by stealth. Set it in the
midst. But do thou, O stranger, say by what name I must call
thee.

ULYSSES

No-man. But obtaining what favor, shall I commend thee?

CYCLOPS

I will banquet on thee the last of all thy companions.

ULYSSES

A pretty honor, indeed, thou grantest to a stranger, O
Cyclops.   426

CYCLOPS

Ho you! what doest thou? art thou drinking the wine by
stealth?

SILENUS

Not so, but this (wine) kissed me, because I look fair.

CYCLOPS

Thou shalt pay for it, kissing the wine that kisses not
thee.   429

SILENUS

Yes, by Jove, since it says that it loves me, being fair.

CYCLOPS
Pour forth, and give me only a full cup.

SILENUS
How is it mixed. Come, let me see.

CYCLOPS
Perdition seize you! give it here.

SILENUS
Not, by Jove, before I see you put on a crown, and I taste it further.

CYCLOPS
My cup-bearer is a cheat.   435

SILENUS
Ay, by Jove, the wine is sweet. But thou oughtest to wipe thy mouth, that thou mayest receive it to drink.

CYCLOPS
See! my lips and beard are clean.

SILENUS
Place then your elbow gracefully, and then drink as thou seest me drinking, or not.

CYCLOPS
Ah! ah! what wilt thou do?   440

SILENUS
I took a delightful draught without drawing breath.

CYCLOPS
Do thou, O stranger, taking it, yourself become my cup-bearer.

ULYSSES
(The juice of) the vine is (well) known to my hand.

CYCLOPS
Come, pour it out then.

ULYSSES
I pour it out; only be silent.   445

CYCLOPS

Thou speakest of a difficult matter to him who drinks much.

ULYSSES

See! taking it, drink it up, and leave nothing. For it behooves a person to take a draught and to die with his cup.

CYCLOPS

O Gods, wise indeed is the tree of the vine.   449

ULYSSES

And if indeed you drink much, in addition to an abundant repast, having moistened your not-thirsting stomach, thou wilt fall asleep. But if thou leavest aught, Bacchus will make thee dry.   452

CYCLOPS

Ho! ho! with what difficulty I have swum out—this is unmixed delight. But the heaven appears to me to be borne along mingled with the earth, and 1 perceive the throne of Jove and all the holy glory of the Gods. I will not kiss you— the Graces are tempting me. Having this Ganymede, enough for me, I shall rest most sweetly, by the Graces. For somehow I am more pleased with boys than women.   458

SILENUS

For am I the Ganymede of Jove, O Cyclops?

CYCLOPS

Ay, by Jove, whom 1 carry off from Dardanus.   460

SILENUS

I am undone, children; I shall suffer wretched ills.

CHORUS

Dost blame thy lover, and wanton over him fallen.

SILENUS

Alas! I soon shall see wine most bitter.

ULYSSES

Come then, ye sons of Bacchus, noble children; the man indeed is within. But relaxed in sleep soon will he vomit forth lumps of flesh from his shameless maw. And the brand sends forth smoke within the hall, and nothing remains to be got ready, but to burn out the Cyclops' eye. Take care then to act like a man.   468

CHORUS

We will have a mind of rock and adamant. But go into the
house, before thy father suffer aught unbeseeming, since
things here are ready for thee.

ULYSSES

O Vulcan, king of Aetna, release thyself at once from thine
evil neighbor, having burnt out his shining eye. And thou
too, sleep, the nursling of black night, fall with thy full
strength upon this God-detested, brute, and do not, after the
most glorious labors of Troy, destroy Ulysses himself, and
his sailors, at the hands of a man who cares naught for Gods
or mortals. Or it is necessary that one esteem fortune a
deity, and the power of the Gods inferior to fortune.   477

CHORUS

Firmly will a crab-like grapple seize the neck of the
feaster on strangers; for by fire he will soon lose his light-
bearing eyes. Already the fire-hardened brand, the mighty
branch of a tree, is hidden in the cinders. But go forth,
Maro, let it maddened work revenge. Let it take out the
Cyclops' eye, that to his cost he may drink. And I desire to
see beloved, ivy-loving Bacchus, quitting the solitude of the
Cyclops. Shall I then come to so great a thing?   484

ULYSSES

By the Gods! be silent, ye savages, keeping close your
mouths, I cannot allow one of you even to breathe, nor wink,
nor cough; lest this evil thing should wake—until that the
sight of the Cyclops' eye be taken away by fire.   487

CHORUS

Let us keep silence, snuffing the air in with your jaws.

ULYSSES

Come then, and seize the brand in your hands, going within.
For it is heated nicely red hot.

CHORUS

You must then appoint those, whom it first behooves to take
the burnt lever, and burn out the eye of the Cyclops, that we
may share in one fortune.

SILENUS

We indeed before the portals are too far off to stand and
drive the fire into his eye.   492

SEMICHORUS
And we have just become lame.

SEMICHORUS
Ye have suffered just the same thing with me; for as we
stood, our feet were convulsed, I know not how.

SEMICHORUS
Ye were convulsed as ye stood?   495

SEMICHORUS
Ay, and our eyes from some where or other are filled with
dust or ashes.

ULYSSES
These allies are worthless cowards, and naught.

CHORUS
Because, forsooth, we have compassion for our back and
spine, and because, being beaten, I do not wish to lose my
teeth, this is cowardice? But I know a most excellent
incantation of Orpheus, so that the brand of its own accord
entering his skull, may burn the one-eyed son of earth.   502

ULYSSES
I have long since known that thou wert such by nature; and
now I know it still better; I needs must then make use of
mine own friends. But if thou hast no strength of hand, at
least cheer (us) on, since we shall obtain courage by the
cheers of you our friends.   506

CHORUS
I will do this. We will run a Carian risk. And as far as
our encouragement goes, let the Cyclops burn. Ho! ho! most
nobly push on, hasten, burn out the eyelid of the monster
that feeds on strangers. Burn, O burn, O the shepherd of
Aetna. Drive, push, lest in his pain lie do you some vain
deed.   511

CYCLOPS
(From within the cave.)
Alas I, I am burnt to ashes as to my bright eye.

CHORUS
Sweet is the paean. Sing this to me, Cyclops.

CYCLOPS
Alas! again, how am I injured, how am I undone!
But ye shall not with impunity escape from out of this
rock, ye men of naught; for standing at the gates of this
opening, I will thus fix my hands.   516

(He comes to the entrance.)

CHORUS
Wherefore dost thou cry out, Cyclops?

CYCLOPS
I am undone.

CHORUS
Ay, thou appearest in base plight.

CYCLOPS
Ay, and wretched to boot.   520

CHORUS
Drunk didst thou fall into the midst of the cinders?

CYCLOPS
No-man has ruined me.

CHORUS
Why, then, no man has harmed thee.

CYCLOPS
No-man has blinded mine eye.

CHORUS
Then thou art not blind.   525

CYCLOPS
As would that you were.

CHORUS
And how could No-man make thee blind?

CYCLOPS
Thou mockest me. But where is No-man?

CHORUS
No where, Cyclops.   529

CYCLOPS
The stranger, that thou mayest rightly know, has destroyed me, the wicked rascal, who having given me the cup, overthrew me.

CHORUS
For wine is terrible, and heavy to strive against.

CYCLOPS
By the Gods, have they escaped, or do they remain within the house?

CHORUS
They stand in silence, having the rock as a shade.

CYCLOPS
At which hand?

535

CHORUS
At thy right.

CYCLOPS
Where?

CHORUS
Close by the rock. Hast thou got them?

CYCLOPS
Evil indeed upon evil! I have struck my skull and broken it.

CHORUS
Ay, and they have escaped thee.

540

CYCLOPS
Not by this road; where you said they were.

CHORUS
I say not by this road.

CYCLOPS
Where then?

CHORUS
They surround thee on your left hand.

CYCLOPS

Alas! I am laughed at; ye mock me in my disaster.   545

CHORUS

But no longer; for this man stands before thee.

CYCLOPS

O thou most base one, where ever art thou?

ULYSSES

Far from thee I am keeping this body of Ulysses under
guard.

CYCLOPS

How sayest thou? changing thy name, dost thou mention a
new one?   549

ULYSSES

Ay, Ulysses, the one my father named me. But thou wast
destined to pay a penalty for thy impious banquets; for in
vain indeed I had burned Troy, had I not avenged on thee the
slaughter of my comrades.   552

CYCLOPS

Alas! the old oracle is fulfilled. For it was said that I
should obtain a blinded sight from thee on thy sailing from
Troy. But it also foretold that thou shouldst undergo
punishment for this, being tossed at sea for a long space of
time.   555

ULYSSES

I bid thee weep! and I have done as I say. But I will go
to the shore, and will launch the bark of my ship upon the
Sicilian Sea, and towards my country.

CYCLOPS

Not so; since breaking off (a piece) of this rock, I will
hurl it, and shatter thee, crew and all. And I will mount
high up on the cliff, although being blind, moving on with my
foot through this crannied rock.

CHORUS

But we indeed, being the fellow-voyagers of Ulysses, will
hereafter serve Bacchus.   561

(EXIT.)

(LIGHTS FADE.)

(CURTAINS.)

(END OF PLAY.)

THE CYCLOPS

A Satyric Drama, from Euripides

Translated by

Percy Bysshe Shelley

CHARACTERS

SILENUS

CHORUS OF SATYRS

ULYSSES

THE CYCLOPS

SILENUS

O Bacchus, what a world of toil, both now
And ere these limbs were overworn with age,
Have I endured for thee! First, when thou fled'st
The mountain-nymphs who nursed thee, driven afar
By the strange madness Juno sent upon thee;
Then in the battle of the Sons of Earth,
When I stood foot by foot close to thy side,
No unpropitious fellow-combatant,
And, driving through his shield my wingèd spear,
Slew vast Enceladus. Consider now,
Is it a dream of which I speak to thee?
By Jove it is not, for you have the trophies!
And now I suffer more than all before.
For when I heard that Juno had devised
A tedious voyage for you, I put to sea
With all my children quaint in search of you,
And I myself stood on the beaked prow,
And fixed the naked mast; and all my boys,
Leaning upon their oars, with splash and strain
Made white with foam the green and purple sea,—
And so we sought you, king. We were sailing
Near Malea, when an eastern wind arose,
And drove us to this waste Aetnean rock;
The one-eyed children of the Ocean God,
The man-destroying Cyclopses, inhabit,
On this wild shore, their solitary caves,
And one of these, named Polypheme, has caught us
To be his slaves; and so, for all delight
Of Bacchic sports, sweet dance and melody,
We keep this lawless giant's wandering flocks.
My sons indeed on far declivities,
Young things themselves, tend on the youngling sheep,
But I remain to fill the water-casks,
Or sweeping the hard floor, or ministering
Some impious and abominable meal
To the fell Cyclops. I am wearied of it!
And now I must scrape up the littered floor
With this great iron rake, so to receive
My absent master and his evening sheep
In a cave neat and clean. Even now I see
My children tending the flocks hitherward.
Ha! what is this? are your Sicinnian measures
Even now the same, as when with dance and song
You brought young Bacchus to Althaea's halls?

CHORUS OF SATYRS

STROPHE

Where has he of race divine   45
   Wandered in the winding rocks?
Here the air is calm and fine
   For the father of the flocks;
Here the grass is soft and sweet,
And the river-eddies meet   50
In the trough beside the cave,
Bright as in their fountain wave.—
Neither here, nor on the dew
   Of the lawny uplands feeding? . . .
Oh, you come!—a stone at you   55
   Will I throw to mend your breeding;—
Get along, you hornèd thing,
Wild, seditious, rambling!

EPODE

An Iacchic melody
   To the golden Aphrodite   60
Will I lift, as erst did I
   Seeking her and her delight
With the Maenads, whose white feet
To the music glance and fleet.
Bacchus, O beloved, where,   65
Shaking wide thy yellow hair,
Wanderest thou alone, afar?
   To the one-eyed Cyclops, we,
Who by right thy servants are,
   Minister in misery,   70
In these wretched goat-skins clad,
   Far from thy delights and thee.

SILENUS

Be silent, sons; command the slaves to drive
The gathered flocks into the rock-roofed cave.

CHORUS

Go! But what needs this serious haste, O father?   75

SILENUS

I see a Grecian vessel on the coast,
And thence the rowers with some general
Approaching to this cave. About their necks
Hang empty vessels, as they wanted food,
And water-flasks.—Oh, miserable strangers!   80
Whence come they, that they know not what and who
My master is, approaching in ill hour

The inhospitable roof of Polypheme,
And the Cyclopian jaw-bone, man-destroying?
Be silent, Satyrs, while I ask and hear
Whence coming, they arrive the Aetnean hill.

ULYSSES

Friends, can you show me some clear water-spring,
The remedy of our thirst? Will any one
Furnish with food seamen in want of it?
Ha! what is this? We seem to be arrived
At the blithe court of Bacchus. I observe
This sportive band of Satyrs near the caves.
First let me greet the elder.—Hail!

SILENUS

Hail thou,
O Stranger! tell thy country and thy race.

ULYSSES

The Ithacan Ulysses and the king Of Cephalonia.

SILENUS

Oh!—I know the man,—
Wordy and shrewd, the son of Sisyphus.

ULYSSES

I am the same, but do not rail upon me.

SILENUS

Whence sailing do you come to Sicily?

ULYSSES

From Ilion, and from the Trojan toils.

SILENUS

How, touched you not at your paternal shore?

ULYSSES

The strength of tempests bore me here by force.

SILENUS

The self-same accident occurred to me.

ULYSSES

Were you then driven here by stress of weather?

                    SILENUS
Following the Pirates who had kidnapped Bacchus.

                    ULYSSES
What land is this, and who inhabit it?

                    SILENUS
Aetna, the loftiest peak in Sicily.

                    ULYSSES
And are there walls, and tower-surrounded towns?

                    SILENUS
There are not. These lone rocks are bare of men.   110

                    ULYSSES
And who possess the land? the race of beasts?

                    SILENUS
Cyclops, who live in caverns, not in houses.

                    ULYSSES
Obeying whom? Or is the state popular?

                    SILENUS
Shepherds no one obeys any in aught.

                    ULYSSES
How live they? do they sow the corn of Ceres?   115

                    SILENUS
On milk and cheese, and on the flesh of sheep.

                    ULYSSES
Have they the Bromian drink from the vine's stream?

                    SILENUS
Ah! no; they live in an ungracious land.

                    ULYSSES
And are they just to strangers?—hospitable?

                    SILENUS
They think the sweetest thing a stranger brings   120
Is his own flesh.

ULYSSES
What! do they eat man's flesh?

SILENUS
No one comes here who is not eaten up.

ULYSSES
The Cyclops now—where is he? Not at home?

SILENUS
Absent on Aetna, hunting with his dogs. 125

ULYSSES
Know'st thou what thou must do to aid us hence?

SILENUS
I know not we will help you all we can.

ULYSSES
Provide us food, of which we are in want.

SILENUS
Here is not anything, as I said, but meat.

ULYSSES
But meat is a sweet remedy for hunger. 130

SILENUS
Cow's milk there is, and store of curdled cheese.

ULYSSES
Bring out; I would see all before I bargain.

SILENUS
But how much gold will you engage to give?

ULYSSES
I bring no gold, but Bacchic juice.

SILENUS
                Oh, joy! 135
Tis long since these dry lips were wet with wine.

ULYSSES
Maron, the son of the God, gave it me.

                    SILENUS
Whom I have nursed a baby in my arms.

                    ULYSSES
The son of Bacchus, for your clearer knowledge.

                    SILENUS
Have you it now?—or is it in the ship?   140

                    ULYSSES
Old man, this skin contains it, which you see.

                    SILENUS
Why, this would hardly be a mouthful for me.

                    ULYSSES
Nay, twice as much as you can draw from thence.

                    SILENUS
You speak of a fair fountain, sweet to me.

                    ULYSSES
Would you first taste of the unmingled wine?   145

                    SILENUS
'Tis just—tasting invites the purchaser.

                    ULYSSES
Here is the cup, together with the skin.

                    SILENUS
Pour; that the draught may fillip my remembrance.

                    ULYSSES
See!

                    SILENUS
      Papaiax! what a sweet smell it has!   150

                    ULYSSES
You see it then?

                    SILENUS
        By Jove, no! but I smell it.

                    ULYSSES
Taste, that you may not praise it in words only.

SILENUS
Babai! Great Bacchus calls me forth to dance!
Joy! joy!

155

ULYSSES
Did it flow sweetly down your throat?

SILENUS
So that it tingled to my very nails.

ULYSSES
And in addition I will give you gold.

SILENUS
Let gold alone! only unlock the cask.

ULYSSES
Bring out some cheeses now, or a young goat.

160

SILENUS
That will I do, despising any master.
Yes, let me drink one cup, and I will give
All that the Cyclops feed upon their mountains.

+++++   +++++

CHORUS
Ye have taken Troy and laid your hands on Helen?

ULYSSES
And utterly destroyed the race of Priam.

165

+++++   +++++

SILENUS
The wanton wretch! she was bewitched to see
The many-coloured anklets and the chain
Of woven gold which girt the neck of Paris,
And so she left that good man Menelaus.
There should be no more women in the world

170

But such as are reserved for me alone.—
See, here are sheep, and here are goats, Ulysses;
Here are unsparing cheeses of pressed milk;
Take them; depart with what good speed ye may;
First leaving my reward, the Bacchic dew

175

Of joy-inspiring grapes.

ULYSSES
      Ah me! Alas!
What shall we do? the Cyclops is at hand!
Old man, we perish! whither can we fly?

SILENUS
Hide yourselves quick within that hollow rock.   180

ULYSSES
'Twere perilous to fly into the net.

SILENUS
The cavern has recesses numberless;
Hide yourselves quick.

ULYSSES
     That will I never do!
The mighty Troy would be indeed disgraced   185
If I should fly one man. How many times
Have I withstood, with shield immovable.
Ten thousand Phrygians!—if I needs must die,
Yet will I die with glory;—if I live,
The praise which I have gained will yet remain.   190

SILENUS
What, ho! assistance, comrades, haste, assistance!

The CYCLOPS, SILENUS, ULYSSES; CHORUS.

CYCLOPS
What is this tumult? Bacchus is not here,
Nor tympanies nor brazen castanets.
How are my young lambs in the cavern? milking
Their dams or playing by their sides? And is   195
The new cheese pressed into the bulrush baskets?
Speak! I'll beat some of you till you rain tears!
Look up, not downwards when I speak to you.

SILENUS
See: I now gape at Jupiter himself;
I stare upon Orion and the stars.   200

CYCLOPS
Well, is the dinner fitly cooked and laid?

SILENUS
All ready, if your throat is ready too.

CYCLOPS
Are the bowls full of milk besides?

SILENUS
O'er-brimming;
So you may drink a tunful if you will.

CYCLOPS
Is it ewe's milk or cow's milk, or both mixed?

SILENUS
Both . . . either . . . Only pray don't swallow me.

CYCLOPS
By no means.—
What is this crowd I see beside the stalls?
Outlaws or thieves? for near my cavern-home
I see my young lambs coupled two by two
With willow bands; mixed with my cheeses lie
Their implements; and this old fellow here
Has his bald head broken with stripes.

SILENUS
Ah me!
I have been beaten till I burn with fever.

CYCLOPS
By whom? Who laid his fist upon your head?

SILENUS
Those men, because I would not suffer them
To steal your goods.

CYCLOPS
Did not the rascals know
I am a God, sprung from the race of Heaven?

SILENUS
I told them so, but they bore-off your things,
And ate the cheese in spite of all I said,
And carried out the lambs: and said, moreover,
They'd pin you down with a three-cubit collar,
And pull your vitals out through your one eye,
Furrow your back with stripes, then, binding you,
Throw you as ballast into the ship's hold,
And then deliver you, a slave, to move
Enormous rocks, or found a vestibule.

                        CYCLOPS
In truth? Nay, haste, and place in order quickly
The cooking-knives, and heap upon the hearth,
And kindle it, a great faggot of wood.—
As soon as they are slaughtered, they shall fill
My belly, broiling warm from the live coals,   235
Or boiled and seethed within the bubbling caldron.
I am quite sick of the wild mountain-game;
Of stags and lions I have gorged enough,
And I grow hungry for the flesh of men.

                        SILENUS
Nay, master, something new is very pleasant   240
After one thing forever, and of late
Very few strangers have approached our cave.

                        ULYSSES
Hear, Cyclops, a plain tale on the other side.
We, wanting to buy food, came from our ship
Into the neighbourhood of your cave, and here   245
This old Silenus gave us in exchange
These lambs for wine, the which he took and drank,
And all by mutual compact, without force.
There is no word of truth in what he says,
For slily he was selling all your store.   250

                        SILENUS
I? May you perish, wretch—

                        ULYSSES
                If I speak false!

                        SILENUS
Cyclops, I swear by Neptune who begot thee,
By mighty Triton and by Nereus old,
Calypso and the glaucous Ocean-Nymphs,   255
The sacred waves and all the race of fishes—
Be these the witnesses, my dear sweet master,
My darling little Cyclops, that I never
Gave any of your stores to these false strangers!
If I speak false may those whom most I love,   260
My children, perish wretchedly!

                        CHORUS
                There stop!
I saw him giving these things to the strangers.
If I speak false, then may my father perish,

But do not thou wrong hospitality.   265

                        CYCLOPS

You lie! I swear that he is juster far
Than Rhadamanthus—I trust more in him.
But let me ask, whence have ye sailed, O strangers?
Who are you? And what city nourished ye?

                        ULYSSES

Our race is Ithacan—having destroyed   270
The town of Troy, the tempests of the sea
Have driven us on thy land, O Polypheme.

                        CYCLOPS

What, have ye shared in the unenvied spoil
Of the false Helen, near Scamander's stream?

                        ULYSSES

The same, having endured a woful toil.   275

                        CYCLOPS

Oh, basest expedition! sailed ye not
From Greece to Phrygia for one woman's sake?

                        ULYSSES

'Twas the Gods' work—no mortal was in fault.—
But, O great Offspring of the Ocean-King!
We pray thee and admonish thee with freedom,   280
That thou dost spare thy friends who visit thee,
And place no impious food within thy jaws.
For in the depths of Greece we have upreared
Temples to thy great Father, which are all
His homes. The sacred bay of Taenarus   285
Remains inviolate, and each dim recess
Scooped high on the Malean promontory,
And aery Sunium's silver-veined crag,
Which divine Pallas keeps unprofaned ever,
The Gerastian asylums, and whate'er   290
Within wide Greece our enterprise has kept
From Phrygian contumely; and in which
You have a common care, for you inhabit
The skirts of Grecian land, under the roots
Of Aetna and its crags, spotted with fire.   295
Turn then to converse under human laws,
Receive us shipwrecked suppliants, and provide
Food, clothes, and fire, and hospitable gifts;
Nor fixing upon oxen-piercing spits

Our limbs, so fill your belly and your jaws.   300
Priam's wide land has widowed Greece enough;
And weapon-winged murder leaped together
Enough of dead, and wives are husbandless,
And ancient women and gray fathers wail
Their childless age. If you should roast the rest   305
(And 'tis a bitter feast that you prepare),
Where then would any turn? Yet be persuaded;
Forgo the lust of your jaw-bone; prefer
Pious humanity to wicked will
Many have bought too dear their evil joys.   310

SILENUS

Let me advise you, do not spare a morsel
Of all his flesh. If you should eat his tongue
You would become most eloquent, O Cyclops.

CYCLOPS

Wealth, my good fellow, is the wise man's God,
All other things are a pretence and boast.   315
What are my father's ocean-promontories,
The sacred rocks whereon he dwells, to me?
Stranger, I laugh to scorn Jove's thunderbolt,
I know not that his strength is more than mine.
As to the rest I care not.—When he pours   320
Rain from above, I have a close pavilion
Under this rock, in which I lie supine,
Feasting on a roast calf or some wild beast,
And drinking pans of milk, and gloriously
Emulating the thunder of high Heaven.   325
And when the Thracian wind pours down the snow,
I wrap my body in the skins of beasts,
Kindle a fire, and bid the snow whirl on.
The earth, by force, whether it will or no,
Bringing forth grass, fattens my flocks and herds,—   330
Which, to what other God but to myself
And this great belly, first of deities,
Should I be bound to sacrifice? I well know
The wise man's only Jupiter is this,
To eat and drink during his little day,   335
And give himself no care. And as for those
Who complicate with laws the life of man,
I freely give them tears for their reward.
I will not cheat my soul of its delight,
Or hesitate in dining upon you.   340
And that I may be quit of all demands,
These are my hospitable gifts; —fierce fire

And yon ancestral caldron, which o'er-bubbling
Shall finely cook your miserable flesh. Creep in!—

+++++   +++++

ULYSSES

Ai! ai! I have escaped the Trojan toils,   345
I have escaped the sea,—and now I fall
Under the cruel grasp of one impious man!
O Pallas, mistress, Goddess, sprung from Jove,
Now, now, assist me! Mightier toils than Troy
Are these;—I totter on the chasms of peril;—   350
And thou who inhabitest the thrones
Of the bright stars, look, hospitable Jove,
Upon this outrage of thy deity,—
Otherwise be considered as no God!

CHORUS
(Alone.)

For your gaping gulf and your gullet wide   355
The ravin is ready on every side,
The limbs of the strangers are cooked and done;
There is boiled meat, and roast meat, and meat
   from the coal,
You may chop it, and tear it, and gnash it for fun;
An hairy goat's-skin contains the whole.   360
Let me but escape, and ferry me o'er
The stream of your wrath to a safer shore.

The Cyclops Aetnean is cruel and bold,
   He murders the strangers
      That sit on his hearth,   365
   And dreads no avengers
      To rise from the earth.
He roasts the men before they are cold,
He snatches them broiling from the coal,
And from the caldron pulls them whole;   370
And minces their flesh and gnaws their bone
With his cursed teeth, till all be gone.

   Farewell, foul pavilion
      Farewell, rites of dread!
   The Cyclops vermilion,   375
   With slaughter uncloying,
      Now feasts on the dead,
 In the flesh of strangers joying!

                    ULYSSES
O Jupiter! I saw within the cave
Horrible things; deeds to be feigned in words,   380
But not to be believed as being done.

                    CHORUS
What! sawest thou the impious Polypheme
Feasting upon your loved companions now?

                    ULYSSES
Selecting two, the plumpest of the crowd,
He grasped them in his hands.—   385

                    CHORUS
          Unhappy man!

               +++++   +++++

                    ULYSSES
Soon as we came into this craggy place,
Kindling a fire, he cast on the broad hearth
The knotty limbs of an enormous oak,
Three waggon-loads at least, and then he strewed   390
Upon the ground, beside the red firelight,
His couch of pine-leaves; and he milked the cows,
And pouring forth the white milk, filled a bowl
Three cubits wide and four in depth, as much
As would contain ten amphorae, and bound it   395
With ivy wreaths; then placed upon the fire
A brazen pot to boil, and made red hot
The points of spits, not sharpened with the sickle
But with a fruit tree bough, and with the jaws
Of axes for Aetnean slaughtering.   400
And when this God-abandoned cook of hell
Had made all ready, he seized two of us
And killed them in a kind of measured manner;—
For he flung one against the brazen rivets
Of the huge caldron, and seized the other   405
By the foot's tendon, and knocked out his brains
Upon the sharp edge of the craggy stone,—
Then peeled his flesh with a great cooking-knife
And put him down to roast. The other's limbs
He chopped into the caldron to be boiled.   410
And I, with the tears raining from my eyes,
Stood near the Cyclops, ministering to him;
The rest, in the recesses of the cave,
Clung to the rock like bats, bloodless with fear.

When he was filled with my companions' flesh,   415
He threw himself upon the ground and sent
A loathsome exhalation from his maw.
Then a divine thought came to me. I filled
The cup of Maron, and I offered him
To taste, and said—"Child of the Ocean God,   420
Behold what drink the vines of Greece produce,
The exultation and the joy of Bacchus."
He, satiated with his unnatural food,
Received it, and at one draught drank it off,
And taking my hand, praised me—"Thou hast given   425
A sweet draught after a sweet meal, dear guest."
And I, perceiving that it pleased him, filled
Another cup, well knowing that the wine
Would wound him soon and take a sure revenge.
And the charm fascinated him, and I   430
Plied him cup after cup, until the drink
Had warmed his entrails, and he sang aloud
In concert with my wailing fellow-seamen
A hideous discord—and the cavern rung.
I have stolen out, so that if you will,   435
You may achieve my safety and your own.
But say, do you desire, or not, to fly
This uncompanionable man, and dwell,
As was your wont among the Grecian Nymphs
Within the fanes of your beloved God?   440
Your father there within agrees to it;
But he is weak and overcome with wine,
And caught as if with birdlime by the cup,
He claps his wings and crows in doting joy.
You who are young escape with me, and find   445
Bacchus your ancient friend; unsuited he
To this rude Cyclops.

CHORUS
           Oh my dearest friend,
That I could see that day, and leave for ever
The impious Cyclops!   450

+++++   +++++

ULYSSES
Listen then what a punishment I have
For this fell monster, how secure a flight
From your hard servitude.

CHORUS

O sweeter far
Than is the music of an Asian lyre   455
Would be the news of Polypheme destroyed!

ULYSSES

Delighted with the Bacchic drink he goes
To call his brother Cyclops—who inhabit
A village upon Aetna not far off.

CHORUS

I understand, catching him when alone   460
You think by some measure to dispatch him,
Or thrust him from the precipice.

ULYSSES

Oh no!
Nothing of that kind; my device is subtle.

CHORUS

How then? I heard of old that thou wert wise.   465

ULYSSES

I will dissuade him from this plan, by saying
It were unwise to give the Cyclopses
This precious drink, which if enjoyed alone
Would make life sweeter for a longer time.
When, vanquished by the Bacchic power, he sleeps,   470
There is a trunk of olive wood within,
Whose point having made sharp with this good sword,
I will conceal in fire, and when I see
It is alight, will fix it, burning yet,
Within the socket of the Cyclops' eye,   475
And melt it out with fire. As when a man
Turns by its handle a great auger round,
Fitting the framework of a ship with beams,
So will I, in the Cyclops' fiery eye
Turn round the brand and dry the pupil up.   480

CHORUS

Joy! I am mad with joy at your device!

ULYSSES

And then with you, my friends, and the old man,
We'll load the hollow depth of our black ship,
And row with double strokes from this dread shore.

CHORUS

May I, as in libations to a God,   485
Share in the blinding him with the red brand?
I would have some communion in his death.

ULYSSES

Doubtless; the brand is a great brand to hold.

CHORUS

Oh! I would lift an hundred waggon-loads,
If like a wasp's nest I could scoop the eye out   490
Of the detested Cyclops.

ULYSSES

          Silence now!
Ye know the close device—and when I call,
Look ye obey the masters of the craft.
I will not save *myself* and leave behind   495
My comrades in the cave I might escape,
Having got clear from that obscure recess,
But 'twere unjust to leave in jeopardy
The dear companions who sailed here with me.

CHORUS

Come! who is first, that with his hand   500
Will urge down the burning brand
Through the lids, and quench and pierce
The Cyclops' eye so fiery fierce?

(A Song is heard within.)

SEMICHORUS I.

Listen! listen! he is coming,   505
A most hideous discord humming.
Drunken, museless, awkward, yelling,
Far along his rocky dwelling;
Let us with some comic spell
Teach the yet unteachable.   510
By all means he must be blinded,
If my counsel be but minded.

SEMICHORUS II.

Happy thou made odorous
With the dew which sweet grapes weep,
To the village hastening thus,   515
Seek the vines that soothe to sleep,
Having first embraced thy friend;
Thou in luxury without end,
With the strings of yellow hair,
Of thy voluptuous leman fair,   520
Shalt sit playing on a bed . . .
Speak! what door is opened?

CYCLOPS

Ha! ha! ha! I'm full of wine,
Heavy with the joy divine,
With the young feast oversated.   525
Like a merchant's vessel freighted
To the water's edge, my crop
Is laden to the gullet's top.
The fresh meadow grass of Spring
Tempts me forth thus wandering   530
    To my brothers on the mountains,
    Who shall share the wine's sweet fountains.
Bring the cask, O stranger, bring!

CHORUS

One with eyes the fairest
  Cometh from his dwelling;   535
Some one loves thee, rarest
  Bright beyond my telling.
In thy grace thou shinest
Like some nymph divinest
In her caverns dewy;—   540
All delights pursue thee!
Soon pied flowers, sweet-breathing,
Shall thy head be wreathing.

ULYSSES
Listen, O Cyclops, for I am well skilled
In Bacchus, whom I gave thee of to drink.   545

CYCLOPS
What sort of God is Bacchus then accounted?

ULYSSES
The greatest among men for joy of life.

CYCLOPS
I gulped him down with very great delight.

ULYSSES
This is a God who never injures men.

CYCLOPS
How does the God like living in a skin?   550

ULYSSES
He is content wherever he is put.

CYCLOPS
Gods should not have their body in a skin.

ULYSSES
If he gives joy, what is his skin to you?

CYCLOPS
I hate the skin, but love the wine within.

ULYSSES
Stay here now drink, and make your spirit glad.   555

CYCLOPS
Should I not share this liquor with my brothers?

ULYSSES
Keep it yourself, and be more honoured so.

CYCLOPS
I were more useful, giving to my friends.

ULYSSES
But village mirth breeds contests, broils, and blows.

CYCLOPS

When I am drunk none shall lay hands on me.   560

                    ULYSSES
A drunken man is better within doors.

                    CYCLOPS
He is a fool, who drinking, loves not mirth.

                    ULYSSES
But he is wise, who drunk, remains at home.

                    CYCLOPS
What shall I do, Silenus? Shall I stay?

                    SILENUS
Stay—for what need have you of pot companions?   565

                    CYCLOPS
Indeed this place is closely carpeted
With flowers and grass.

                    SILENUS
            And in the sun-warm noon
'Tis sweet to drink. Lie down beside me now,
Placing your mighty sides upon the ground.   570

                    CYCLOPS
What do you put the cup behind me for?

                    SILENUS
That no one here may touch it.

                    CYCLOPS
            Thievish One!
You want to drink;—here place it in the midst.
And thou, O stranger, tell how art thou called?   575

                    ULYSSES
My name is Nobody. What favour now
Shall I receive to praise you at your hands?

                    CYCLOPS
I'll feast on you the last of your companions.

                    ULYSSES
You grant your guest a fair reward, O Cyclops.

CYCLOPS

Ha! what is this? Stealing the wine, you rogue!   580

SILENUS

It was this stranger kissing me because
I looked so beautiful.

CYCLOPS

            You shall repent
For kissing the coy wine that loves you not.

SILENUS

By Jupiter! you said that I am fair.   585

CYCLOPS

Pour out, and only give me the cup full.

SILENUS

How is it mixed? Let me observe.

CYCLOPS

            Curse you!
Give it me so.

SILENUS

      Not till I see you wear   590
That coronal, and taste the cup to you.

CYCLOPS

Thou wily traitor!

SILENUS

      But the wine is sweet.
Ay, you will roar if you are caught in drinking.

CYCLOPS

See now, my lip is clean and all my beard.   595

SILENUS

Now put your elbow right and drink again.
As you see me drink— . . .

CYCLOPS

How now?

SILENUS

      Ye Gods, what a delicious gulp!

CYCLOPS
Guest, take it;—you pour out the wine for me.   600

ULYSSES
The wine is well accustomed to my hand.

CYCLOPS
Pour out the wine!

ULYSSES
I pour; only be silent.

CYCLOPS
Silence is a hard task to him who drinks.

ULYSSES
Take it and drink it off; leave not a dreg.   605
                    (Aside.)
Oh that the drinker died with his own draught!

CYCLOPS
Papai! the vine must be a sapient plant.

ULYSSES
If you drink much after a mighty feast,
Moistening your thirsty maw, you will sleep well;
If you leave aught, Bacchus will dry you up.   610

CYCLOPS
Ho! ho! I can scarce rise. What pure delight!
The heavens and earth appear to whirl about
Confusedly. I see the throne of Jove
And the clear congregation of the Gods.   615
Now if the Graces tempted me to kiss
I would not, for the loveliest of them all
I would not leave this Ganymede.

SILENUS
                    Polypheme,
I am the Ganymede of Jupiter.   620

CYCLOPS
By Jove, you are; I bore you off from Dardanus.

+++++   +++++

ULYSSES and the CHORUS

ULYSSES

Come, boys of Bacchus, children of high race!
This man within is folded up in sleep,
And soon will vomit flesh from his fell maw;
The brand under the shed thrusts out its smoke,   625
No preparation needs, but to burn out
The monster's eye;—but bear yourselves like men.

CHORUS

We will have courage like the adamant rock,
All things are ready for you here; go in,
Before our father shall perceive the noise.   630

ULYSSES

Vulcan, Aetnean king! burn out with fire
The shining eye of this thy neighbouring monster!
And thou, O Sleep, nursling of gloomy Night,
Descend unmixed on this God-hated beast!
And suffer not Ulysses and his comrades,   635
Returning from their famous Trojan toils,
To perish by this man, who cares not either
For God or mortal; or I needs must think
That Chance is a supreme divinity,
And things divine are subject to her power.   640

CHORUS

Soon a crab the throat will seize
   Of him who feeds upon his guest,—
Fire will burn his lamp-like eyes
   In revenge of such a feast!
A great oak-stump now is lying   645
In the ashes yet undying.
   Come, Maron, come!
Raging let him fix the doom,
Let him tear the eyelid up
Of the Cyclops—that his cup   650
   May be evil!
Oh! I long to dance and revel
With sweet Bromian, long desired,
In loved ivy wreaths attired;
Leaving this abandoned home—   655
Will the moment ever come?

ULYSSES

Be silent, ye wild things! Nay, hold your peace,

And keep your lips quite close; dare not to breathe,
Or spit, or e'en wink, lest ye wake the monster,
Until his eye be tortured out with fire. 660

CHORUS
Nay, we are silent, and we chaw the air.

ULYSSES
Come now, and lend a hand to the great stake within—it is
delightfully red hot.

CHORUS
You then command who first should seize the stake
To burn the Cyclops' eye, that all may share
In the great enterprise.

SEMICHORUS I.
We are too far; 665
We cannot at this distance from the door
Thrust fire into his eye.

SEMICHORUS II.
And we just now
Have become lame! cannot move hand or foot.

CHORUS
The same thing has occurred to us,—our ankles 670
Are sprained with standing here, I know not how.

ULYSSES
What, sprained with standing still?

CHORUS
And there is dust
Or ashes in our eyes, I know not whence.

ULYSSES
Cowardly dogs! ye will not aid me then? 675

CHORUS
With pitying my own back and my back-bone,
And with not wishing all my teeth knocked out,
This cowardice comes of itself. But stay!
I know a famous Orphic incantation
To make the brand stick of its own accord 680
Into the skull of this one-eyed Son of Earth.

ULYSSES
Of old I knew ye thus by nature; now
I know ye better.—I will use the aid
Of my own comrades.—Yet though weak of hand
Speak cheerfully, that so ye may awaken   685
The courage of my friends with your blithe words.

CHORUS
This I will do with peril of my life,
And blind you with my exhortations, Cyclops.

   Hasten and thrust,
   And parch up to dust,   690
   The eye of the beast
   Who feeds on his guest.
   Burn and blind
   The Aetnean hind!
   Scoop and draw,   695
   But beware lest he claw
   Your limbs near his maw.

CYCLOPS
Ah me! my eyesight is parched up to cinders!

CHORUS
What a sweet paean! sing me that again!

CYCLOPS
Ah me! indeed, what woe has fallen upon me?   700
But, wretched nothings, think ye not to flee
Out of this rock; I, standing at the outlet,
Will bar the way and catch you as you pass.

CHORUS
What are you roaring out, Cyclops?

CYCLOPS
   I perish!   705

CHORUS
For you are wicked.

CYCLOPS
   And besides miserable.

CHORUS
What, did you fall into the fire when drunk?

CYCLOPS
'Twas Nobody destroyed me.

CHORUS
                Why then no one
Can be to blame.

CYCLOPS
                I say 'twas Nobody
Who blinded me.

CHORUS
        Why then you are not blind.

CYCLOPS
I wish you were as blind as I am!

CHORUS
                Nay,
It cannot be that no one made you blind.

CYCLOPS
You jeer me; where, I ask, is Nobody?

CHORUS
No-where, O Cyclops.

CYCLOPS
It was that stranger ruined me—the wretch
First gave me wine and then burned out my eye,
For wine is strong and hard to struggle with.
Have they escaped, or are they yet within?

CHORUS
They stand under the darkness of the rock
And cling to it.

CYCLOPS
At my right hand or left?

CHORUS
Close on your right.

CYCLOPS

Where?

CHORUS

Near the rock itself.
You have them.

CYCLOPS

Oh, misfortune on misfortune!
I've cracked my skull.

CHORUS

Now they escape you there.

CYCLOPS

Not there, although you say so.

CHORUS

Not on that side.

CYCLOPS

Where then?

CHORUS

They creep about you on your left.

CYCLOPS

Ah! I am mocked! They jeer me in my ills.

CHORUS

Not there! he is a little there beyond you.

CYCLOPS

Detested wretch! where are you?

ULYSSES

Far from you
I keep with care this body of Ulysses.

CYCLOPS

What do you say? You proffer a new name.

ULYSSES

My father named me so; and I have taken
A full revenge for your unnatural feast;
I should have done ill to have burned down Troy
And not revenged the murder of my comrades.

CYCLOPS
Ai! ai! the ancient oracle is accomplished;
It said that I should have my eyesight blinded
By your coming from Troy, yet it foretold   750
That you should pay the penalty for this
By wandering long over the homeless sea.

ULYSSES
I bid thee weep!—consider what I say;
I go towards the shore to drive my ship
To mine own land, o'er the Sicilian wave.   755

CYCLOPS
Not so, if, whelming you with this huge stone,
I can crush you and all your men together!
I will descend upon the shore, though blind,
Groping my way adown the steep ravine.

CHORUS
And we, the shipmates of Ulysses now,
Will serve our Bacchus all our happy lives.   761

(Exit.)

(LIGHT FADE.)

(CURTAINS.)

(END OF PLAY.)